DISCOVERING VOICE

Lessons to Teach Reading and Writing of Complex Text

By Nancy Dean

Maupin House *by*
capstone professional

Discovering Voice: Lessons to Teach Reading and Writing of Complex Text

By Nancy Dean

Cover Design: Sandra D'Antonio

Book Design: Lisa King

Photo Credits: Shutterstock: cover; konradrza, 122

Library of Congress Cataloging-in-Publication Data

Cataloging-in-publication information is on file with the Library of Congress.

978-1-62521-933-6 (pbk.)
978-1-62521-943-5 (eBook PDF)
978-1-4966-0055-4 (eBook)

Maupin House publishes professional resources for K–12 educators. Contact us for tailored, in-school training or to schedule an author for a workshop or conference. Visit www.maupinhouse.com for free lesson plan downloads.

Maupin House Publishing, Inc. by Capstone Professional
1710 Roe Crest Drive
North Mankato, MN 56003

www.maupinhouse.com

888-262-6135

info@maupinhouse.com

Printed in the United States of America in Eau Claire, Wisconsin.

012015   008739

Dedication

To the students who share their voices with us, their teachers.

Acknowledgments

A special thanks to Christy Gabbard, Jen Cheveallier, and Greg Cunningham, extraordinary educators at P.K. Yonge Developmental Research School. I deeply appreciate your encouragement and support.

A heartfelt thanks to Karen Soll of Capstone Professional for her sensitive reading of this manuscript. Her insights and persistence enhanced every aspect of this book.

To the teachers who have found *Discovering Voice* useful over the years: Thank you for sharing your comments and expertise with me.

To Tom, who throws quotes at me and is never too busy to discuss them: Nothing makes sense without you.

Table of Contents

Preface to the Second Edition

The world of education has changed since 2006, when *Discovering Voice* was first published. With the introduction of the Common Core State Standards (CCSS) initiative, teachers have seen increased emphasis on accountability, college- and career-readiness skills for students, and high expectations for students' reading and writing. At the center of these changes are the key shifts in English language arts (Copyright 2010. National Governors Association Center for Best Practices and Council of Chief State School Officers. All rights reserved.). These include practice with complex texts; reading, writing, and speaking grounded in evidence from text; and building knowledge through content-rich nonfiction. Although the standards are clear and carefully written, many teachers are uncertain just how to help their students make the shifts requisite for implementation. In my work with teachers, I am asked again and again for activities that guide students as they make the key shifts and implement CCSS College- and Career-Readiness Standards. My hope is that the new edition of *Discovering Voice* will fill this need.

Practice with Complex Text

To address the need for practice with complex text, the new edition of *Discovering Voice* includes many new quotations—quotations that are quite challenging in terms of vocabulary, structure, language, and levels of meaning. These exemplary quotations are short, so students can learn how to manage close reading of complex text without being overwhelmed by a long passage. Although they are short, the quotations are certainly worth students' time and effort. Students can learn the value of reading and rereading, discovering how to examine complex text fully and deeply. The quotations and the questions that follow help bring students to an understanding of how complex text works and how to read closely for both comprehension and appreciation of great writing.

Reading, Writing, and Speaking Grounded in Evidence from Text

To address the need for evidence, the new *Discovering Voice* pays careful attention to the call for students to base their answers on evidence from the text. As teachers help students read closely and fully then model what they have learned, students discover how to analyze text by grounding their observations in evidence. Students practice evidence-based reading, writing, and speaking through an examination of the elements of voice (diction, detail, figurative language, imagery, syntax, and tone) in the quotations. With practice, students discover how to support their observations with evidence, searching through complex text for a full understanding of what a text says and how it works.

Building Knowledge through Content-Rich Nonfiction

Finally, the new *Discovering Voice* addresses content-rich nonfiction by including many new nonfiction quotations for students to examine. These include speeches, science writing, autobiographies, letters, and travel accounts. Further, the new edition provides students with ample opportunities to build knowledge through their own reading and writing. This necessitates students working with text rather than being told about it by the teacher. The voice activities in this edition encourage students to read and reread and to work with text on their own. By examining the elements of voice in well-written, nonfiction text, students will come to the understanding that nonfiction—like fiction—has voice and that they can acquire a deep understanding and appreciation of nonfiction.

College and Career Readiness Anchor Standards Addressed in *Discovering Voice*

In addition to addressing the key shifts in English language arts, *Discovering Voice* addresses the following English Language Arts Anchor Standards (Copyright 2010. National Governors Association Center for Best Practices and Council of Chief State School Officers. All rights reserved.):

College and Career Readiness Anchor Standards for Reading

CCSS.ELA-Literacy.CCRA.R.1: Read closely to determine what the text says explicitly and to make logical inferences from it; cite specific textual evidence when writing or speaking to support conclusions drawn from the text.

CCSS.ELA-Literacy.CCRA.R.2: Determine central ideas or themes of a text and analyze their development; summarize the key supporting details and ideas.

CCSS.ELA-Literacy.CCRA.R.4: Interpret words and phrases as they are used in a text, including determining technical, connotative, and figurative meanings, and analyze how specific word choices shape meaning or tone.

CCSS.ELA-Literacy.CCRA.R.5: Analyze the structure of texts, including how specific sentences, paragraphs, and larger portions of the text (e.g., a section, chapter, scene, or stanza) relate to each other and the whole.

CCSS.ELA-Literacy.CCRA.R.6: Assess how point of view or purpose shapes the content and style of a text.

CCSS.ELA-Literacy.CCRA.R.10: Read and comprehend complex literary and informational texts independently and proficiently.

College and Career Readiness Anchor Standards for Writing

CCSS.ELA-Literacy.CCRA.W.3: Write narratives to develop real or imagined experiences or events using effective technique, well-chosen details, and well-structured event sequences.

CCSS.ELA-Literacy.CCRA.W.4: Produce clear and coherent writing in which the development, organization, and style are appropriate to task, purpose, and audience.

CCSS.ELA-Literacy.CCRA.W.5: Develop and strengthen writing as needed by planning, revising, editing, rewriting, or trying a new approach.

CCSS.ELA-Literacy.CCRA.W.9: Draw evidence from literary or informational texts to support analysis, reflection, and research.

CCSS.ELA-Literacy.CCRA.W.10: Write routinely over extended time frames (time for research, reflection, and revision) and shorter time frames (a single sitting or a day or two) for a range of tasks, purposes, and audiences.

College and Career Readiness Anchor Standards for Speaking and Listening

CCSS.ELA-Literacy.CCRA.SL.1: Prepare for and participate effectively in a range of conversations and collaborations with diverse partners, building on others' ideas and expressing their own clearly and persuasively.

College and Career Readiness Anchor Standards for Language

CCSS.ELA-Literacy.CCRA.L.1: Demonstrate command of the conventions of standard English grammar and usage when writing or speaking.

CCSS.ELA-Literacy.CCRA.L.2: Demonstrate command of the conventions of standard English capitalization, punctuation, and spelling when writing.

CCSS.ELA-Literacy.CCRA.L.3: Apply knowledge of language to understand how language functions in different contexts, to make effective choices for meaning or style, and to comprehend more fully when reading or listening.

CCSS.ELA-Literacy.CCRA.L.4: Determine or clarify the meaning of unknown and multiple-meaning words and phrases by using context clues, analyzing meaningful word parts, and consulting general and specialized reference materials, as appropriate.

CCSS.ELA-Literacy.CCRA.L.5: Demonstrate understanding of figurative language, word relationships, and nuances in word meanings.

I hope you find the new *Discovering Voice* helpful as you prepare your students for the demands of the 21st century. May your students learn that studying difficult text is good exercise for the mind. It makes our brains grow stronger and builds endurance for the many challenging tasks life throws at us.

Nancy Dean

To the Teacher

Discovering Voice is a book about *voice*, that elusive quality that makes reading interesting and writing distinctive. The study of voice helps students understand the power of language and the tools of the writer. It helps them read closely and deeply.

Voice is central to all communication. It is the expression of who we are, the fingerprint of our language. Studying voice gives students an appreciation for the richness of words and a deep insight into reading. Indeed, voice study helps students become fully literate. We want that for all of our students.

The goal of *Discovering Voice* is for all students to understand voice in their reading and to develop a strong, personal voice in their writing. To do this, we need to provide accessible examples of the elements of voice—diction, detail, figurative language, imagery, syntax, and tone—used effectively. And we need to show students how they can apply the elements of voice to their own writing. That is what *Discovering Voice* is all about.

Discovering Voice is a teacher resource book for students in middle and high school, a collection of lessons and activities to teach close reading and the elements of voice. Each lesson in this book has

- a quotation from fiction or nonfiction written by the experts,
- two discussion questions that direct students' attention to an analysis of a specific element of voice, and
- an application exercise that encourages students to put what they have learned into practice by modeling the quotation in their own writing.

In addition, *Discovering Voice* offers a collection of challenging quotes that students can use to write their own voice lessons (another way to increase understanding) and a sampling of additional activities for teaching voice.

Discovering Voice is not a complete curriculum. It is designed to supplement the regular English or reading curriculum. I recommend using the lessons two or three times a week as class openers to stimulate interest in the critical reading of complex text, the understanding of how great writers use voice, and the development of personal voice in writing. You may photocopy the lessons and the section introductions for classes of students, as specified in the copyright agreement; or you may display the quotations and have students complete the exercises on their own paper. However you decide to use the lessons, it is important to remember that students need the support of having the quotation in front of them for analysis and as a model for their own writing.

Each lesson will take between 10 and 20 minutes, depending on the lesson's difficulty and student interest. Each lesson is complete in itself, and the order of lessons is flexible. I do recommend, however, that you go through at least one cycle of lessons from the diction, detail, figurative language, imagery, and syntax sections before you approach tone. Understanding tone requires a basic knowledge of the other voice elements. I like to teach two or three lessons from each category, then go back and start again. For example, I would teach the introduction and two lessons from the diction, detail, figurative language, imagery, syntax, and tone sections (over a period of about 10 weeks), then start over again to reinforce the skills and concepts.

To hold students accountable for the lessons, I recommend requiring students to take notes on the "Talk about it" discussions and to write out their "Now you try it" responses. I also recommend collecting their work once a week to check it over. Much of the work is oral, so written teacher feedback is minimal. My goal is to give teachers a practical classroom resource that does not increase teacher workload.

I have included suggestions for answering the discussion questions in the back of this book (starting on page 119). These are my suggestions only and by no means exhaust the possible responses to the questions. My intent is to spark discussion and encourage thinking. I fully acknowledge and recognize you, the classroom teacher, as the expert, and I honor your ideas and insights.

I hope that the new Discovering Voice is helpful, interesting, and challenging for you and your students. I wish you well as you help shape your students' voices.

To the Student

This book is about *voice*. After completing the activities, you will learn how to recognize voice in reading and writing. You will learn the elements that make up voice in reading and writing. You will learn to write with a clear voice of your own. So what's voice, anyway?

Voice is what makes reading interesting. It's what makes us say, "I'll bet that story is by Edgar Allen Poe or Stephen King." Voice is what gives color and texture to communication and keeps us interested. Voice is also important in visual arts and in music. When you see a painting and know immediately that it is by van Gogh or Picasso, you are tuning in to voice. When you hear a song and know who is singing in the first few seconds, you are paying attention to voice. Voice is the expression of personality, the fingerprint of creativity. Voice can be strong and distinctive or reserved and generic, but all communication has voice of some kind.

Voice is created through *conscious choices*. In other words, the writer, painter, or musician purposefully chooses his or her "tools" (words, colors, instruments) and uses them in ways that create a certain effect. You will learn more about this as we look deeper into voice in reading and writing, but always remember that the creation of voice involves conscious choices. As you consider the conscious choices writers, painters, or musicians make, learn to ask yourself some fundamental questions:

1. What is he/she (or the work) saying? (What does the work mean?)

2. How do you know? (What evidence can you find in the work to determine the meaning?)

3. How does he/she do that? (What tools does the writer/painter/musician use to create meaning, and how does he/she use these tools?)

These questions will guide your thinking and focus your attention on the elements of voice and the conscious choices people make as they create works of art—with words, lines, or sounds.

In this book, we will focus on understanding voice in reading and creating voice in writing. It may seem difficult at first, but you will find it gets easier with practice, like everything else. As you go through the exercises of the book, we'll use a standard format. We'll start with a passage to read and think about ("Read and think"). Then you'll consider and discuss the answers to two questions about the passage ("Talk about it"). These are not comprehension questions. (We will assume you understand the passages; but if you don't, read the passage again slowly to understand what the author is saying.) Instead, the questions direct you to the aspect of voice we are considering. The questions will help you understand how the passage works, how the writing creates an effect or causes a certain response in the reader. You will discuss the questions with your teacher and classmates, as a whole class or in groups. Finally, you will try your hand at creating your own clear voice in writing, using the specific passage as a model ("Now you try it").

Sometimes voice in reading and writing is hard to understand. We're just not used to thinking about reading and writing in this way. To help you get started, we'll begin our study of voice by looking at visual art since we are used to getting insights into personality by watching people's looks, gestures, and choices of clothing. A visual artist expresses voice through the conscious choice of lines, colors, shading, foreground/background, and detail.

Introduction to Voice

Look and think:

Examine a self-portrait by Vincent van Gogh, a famous artist. You can find examples of his self-portraits online. Think about how van Gogh expresses his voice—his style or personality. Look carefully at the details of van Gogh's self-portrait.

Talk about it:

1. What is van Gogh saying about himself? Complete these two statements as if you were the van Gogh of this portrait.

I am...

I feel...

Base your statements on the picture, not your own feelings. Share your statements with the class.

2. How do you know what van Gogh is saying about himself? What evidence can you find in the picture that supports your statements?

Now you try it:

Think about how you would paint a self-portrait. What colors would you use? What expression would you have on your face? How would you be dressed? What kind of background would you have? Would you have anything else in the picture beside yourself? What would these choices say about you? Make a simple sketch of your self-portrait, and write a few sentences describing what you would like your self-portrait to look like.

Introduction to Voice

Look and think:

Examine a self-portrait by Marc Chagall, another famous artist. Think about how he expresses his voice—his style or personality. Look carefully at the details of Chagall's self-portrait. Again, you can find copies of his self-portraits on the Internet.

Talk about it:

1. What is Chagall saying about himself? Complete these two statements as if you were the Chagall of this portrait.

   I am…

   I feel…

   Base your statements on the picture, not on your own feelings. Share your statements with the class.

2. How do you know what Chagall is saying about himself? What evidence can you find in the picture that supports your statements? Now consider the question: How does he do that? How does Chagall control voice in his painting?

Now you try it:

Compare and contrast van Gogh's and Chagall's self-portraits. Use a Venn diagram (intersecting circles showing what qualities are unique to each artist and what qualities are the same) to show how the self-portraits are similar and how they are different. Be certain to focus on the **choices** the artists make.

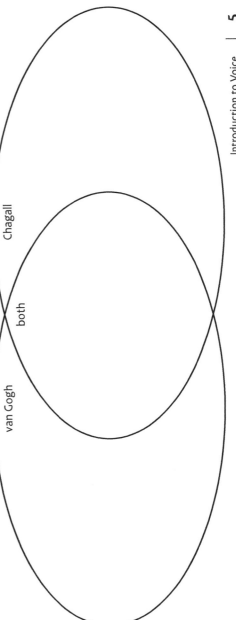

van Gogh | both | Chagall

Introduction to Voice

Musicians have voice too. Like visual artists, musicians make conscious choices in order to create an effect. Musicians choose the kinds of instruments they will use, how fast or slow the music is, and whether it is high or low, loud or soft.

Listen and think:

Listen carefully to the first three to five minutes of *Adagio for Strings*, Op. 11 by Samuel Barber or another very subdued instrumental piece, and think about its voice.

Talk about it:

1. What kind of voice does this music have? Pretend the music is a kind of self-portrait. Write two statements that capture the voice of this "self-portrait."

   I am...

   I feel....

2. What evidence can you find in the music to support your statements? Be specific. Remember that the composer had choices, and he made conscious decisions.

Now you try it:

Pretend that you are a composer. What kind of music would you write to express your personality? What kinds of instruments would you use? What kinds of rhythm would you use? What about volume? Write a paragraph describing the music you would write to express your personality. What do these choices reveal about you? Think carefully about the choices you would make.

Introduction to Voice

Listen and think:

Listen carefully to the first three to five minutes of Beethoven's *Fifth Symphony* or another rousing and grand piece of instrumental music, and think about its voice.

Talk about it:

1. What kind of voice does this music have? How is it different from Barber's voice? Pretend the music is a kind of self-portrait. Write two statements that capture the voice of this "self-portrait."

   I am...

   I feel...

2. What evidence can you find in the music to support your statements? Be specific. Try to focus on one instrument at a time, and think about tempo (how fast the music goes) and volume.

Now you try it:

Bring in some of your favorite music to share with the class. Listen to the music, write self-portrait statements about the music, and discuss the evidence that supports your statements.

Introduction to Voice

Now let's think about voice in reading and writing. Writers make conscious choices too, and good readers learn to recognize and understand the effects of these choices. These choices create voice. Let's start with a very simple sentence.

Read and think:

The little pink fishes swam upstream and died.

Talk about it:

1. Is this sentence sad? Think about this carefully. Don't focus on the idea of a dying fish. Instead, focus on the sentence itself and the effect it produces. Does the sentence make you feel sad or like crying when you read it? Why or why not?

2. Most people will agree that the sentence is not very sad. Why? What specific characteristics in the sentence keep it from being sad? As you identify these characteristics, you are beginning to look at the tools writers have to choose from as they create voice.

Now you try it:

Write a sad version of the sentence, "The little pink fishes swam upstream and died." What did you do to make it sad? In other words, what conscious choices did you make? As you make this sentence sad, you are on your way to using voice in your writing.

Elements of Voice

Writing with a clear voice doesn't just happen; it requires conscious choices. To appreciate voice in reading and to write with your own clear voice, you have to understand and practice the basic elements of voice:

- Diction
- Detail
- Figurative language
- Imagery
- Syntax
- Tone

Diction refers to the choice of words and is the foundation of voice and all good writing. **Detail** refers to the facts, observations, and incidents that develop a topic. Writing is flat and boring without detail. **Figurative language** is the use of words in an unusual way to reveal new meaning, meaning that is not literal and makes the reader think. **Imagery** is the use of words to capture a sensory experience (what you hear, see, smell, taste, or touch). Imagery brings life to what you write and makes it seem real. **Syntax** includes sentence structure, word order, and punctuation. Controlling syntax is one way to express ideas and thoughts in a fully developed, mature way. Writers express tone through the use of diction, detail, imagery, figurative language, and syntax. Finally, **tone** is the expression of attitude in writing. We will consider each of these elements of voice separately as we explore voice and provide practice in the exercises that follow.

In the following pages, you will learn more about the elements of voice and how famous writers use these elements. You will also learn how to express your own voice clearly in writing. Don't expect to master everything at once, but you will learn to think about reading and writing differently as you work through the exercises of this book. Good luck to you as you learn to model and master voice lessons. May the conscious choices you make ring strong and true.

Diction

Introduction

Diction refers to the author's choice of words. Words are the basic tools of the writer. Just as a painter uses color and light or a musician uses sounds and rhythm, a writer uses words. In order to write well, you have to find the perfect word.

The perfect word is clear, concrete, and exact: It says exactly what you want it to say, is specific, and creates just the picture you see in your mind. A character doesn't just "look for" something; she "rummages." You don't "hang" around the house; you "mope" around the house. The perfect word perfectly expresses the feeling or idea you want to get across. It is not always easy to find the perfect word, however. If the word you already know isn't the perfect word, stretch yourself a little. Ask someone for a better word. Look up the word you know in a dictionary and search for synonyms. Or you can try a thesaurus, one of the writer's most valuable tools.

Some words are especially overused and tired, certainly not perfect. These words have lost their freshness and impact. Avoid them at all times. Below is a short list of words that you should avoid. They are general, abstract words that create no clear picture in the reader's mind. Consider these "Forbidden Words" and eliminate them from your written vocabulary. You'll be a better writer for it.

Forbidden Words

good

nice

pretty

beautiful

fine

bad

thing

really

very

terrible

wonderful

a lot

As you study diction and improve your vocabulary, you may want to add more words to the "Forbidden Words" list.

Words don't simply have meaning. Words also have denotation and connotation. Denotation is the literal meaning of the word, and connotation is the meaning suggested by a word, the feeling evoked by a word. It's important to know both aspects of a word's meaning. For example, the words "ambitious" and "eager" have roughly the same denotation: desirous of reaching a goal. However, the connotations of these words are quite different. "Ambitious" carries with it the feeling of wanting something for selfish reasons and with a determination that sometimes ignores the effects of actions on others. "Eager" has a different connotation altogether: a feeling of enthusiasm and fresh-faced optimism. It is a more positive word. When you are thinking about diction, it is important to consider the full meaning of a word.

Words can be formal or informal, depending on the writer's audience and purpose. Just as you talk differently to your friends and your teachers, writers choose different words depending on whom they are writing for and why. If you are writing a letter to your school principal to convince him or her that your opinion about school uniforms is the correct one, you should use formal, strong, and specific words with clearly understood meanings. If, on the other hand, you are writing a short story to be read by people your own age, you might want to use slang and lots of teen dialect. A writer's words should always suit the audience and purpose of the piece.

Effective diction gives freshness, originality, and precision to writing. When you use words in surprising and unusual ways, you have the power to make people think, laugh, or examine new ideas. When you use words in precise and technical ways, you have the power to help people understand difficult concepts. That's a gift and a responsibility. Learn to experiment and play with words. You need a good vocabulary in order to be a good writer.

Diction

(Note that words have been boldfaced for my emphasis in this section's passages.)

Read and think:

The snow came on. The wind **twisted** all day and all night and all the next day. The wind **changed black** and twisted and **spit** icicles in their faces. They **got** lost in the blizzard.

Carl Sandburg, "How the Five Rusty Rats Helped Find a New Village," *Rootabaga Stories*

Talk about it:

1. What does "the wind changed black" mean? How does this unusual use of a color word help you visualize the scene?

2. How would the meaning of Sandburg's sentences change if we changed some of the words? For example:

   The wind blew all day and all night and all the next day. The wind changed direction and blew icicles in their faces.

Now you try it:

Write a sentence describing an unbearably hot day, using Sandburg's sentences as a model. Choose words that are clear, concrete, and exact. Start a collection of "perfect" words you can use later in your writing.

Perfect Words

Perfect action words (verbs)	Perfect words to describe something (adjectives)
Example: instead of "stand," use "slouch"	*Example:* instead of "pretty," use "haunting"

Diction

Read and think:

She knew a small side door which she could unbolt herself and she **flew** down-stairs in her stocking feet and put on her shoes in the hall. She unchained and unbolted and unlocked and when the door was open she **sprang** across the step with one bound, and there she was standing on the grass, which seemed to have turned green, and with the sun **pouring down on her** and warm sweet wafts about her and the fluting and twittering and singing coming from every bush and tree.

Frances Hodgson Burnett, *The Secret Garden*

Talk about it:

1. What does it mean to say someone "flew" downstairs and "sprang" across a step? Think carefully about the denotative and connotative meanings of those words.

2. In this paragraph, does having "the sun pouring down on her" have a positive or negative connotation? How do you know?

Now you try it:

Write a sentence describing someone going outside in the first snowfall of the year. Be sure your sentence has a positive connotation. Use Burnett's sentence as a model. Add any "perfect" words you and your classmates find to your "Perfect Words" list.

Diction

Read and think:

From time to time they sped by some phantom-like tree, whose **white skeleton** twisted and rattled in the wind. Sometimes flocks of wild birds rose, or bands of **gaunt, famished,** ferocious prairie-wolves ran howling after the sledge*.

Jules Verne, *Around the World in Eighty Days*

*sled or sleigh

Talk about it:

1. We usually think of a skeleton as belonging to an animal. Here, Verne uses the word "skeleton" to describe a tree. What does it mean for a tree to have a skeleton, and why is the skeleton white? How does this use of diction help the reader visualize the scene?

2. The second sentence describes a pack of fierce wolves chasing the sled. How do the words "gaunt" and "famished" intensify the understanding of just how ferocious the wolves are?

Now you try it:

Write down two strong adjectives that intensify the reader's understanding of the dogs in the following sentence:

A group of _____, _____, sleepy dogs sat lounging in the shade.

Diction

Read and think:

With the aurora borealis **flaming coldly** overhead, or the stars leaping in the frost dance, and the land numb and frozen under its pall of snow, this song of the huskies might have been the **defiance of life**, only it was pitched in minor key, with long-drawn wailings and half-sobs, and was more the **pleading of life**, the articulate travail of existence.

Jack London, The Call of the Wild

Talk about it:

1. How can something be "flaming coldly"? It seems like a senseless contradiction at first. Upon looking closer, though, it makes sense. How does this odd diction help the reader understand the scene? (If you don't know what the aurora borealis is, please look it up. You need to know this in order to answer the question.)

2. London describes the "song of the huskies" as the "pleading of life" not the "defiance of life." What does this mean and what diction in the passage supports this argument?

Now you try it:

Fill in the blanks below with words that seem to contradict each other but nevertheless add depth and meaning to the sentence. Use London's first sentence as a model.

Her temper was _____ (use an -ing form of a verb) _____ (use an -ly adverb to describe the verb) when she heard the man scream at the dog.

Diction

Read and think:

They **scuttled** for days and days and days till they came to a great forest, 'sclusively full of trees and bushes and stripy, speckly, **patchy-blatchy** shadows, and there they hid: and after another long time, what with standing half in the shade and half out of it, and what with the **slippery-slidy** shadows of the trees falling on them, the Giraffe grew blotchy, and the Zebra grew stripy, and Eland the Koodoo grew darker...

Rudyard Kipling, "How the Leopard Got His Spots," *Just So Stories*

Talk about it:

1. What is the dictionary definition of "scuttled"? How would your mental picture change if the passage said, *They **trudged** for days and days...?*

2. Consider the hyphenated adjectives Kipling uses in this passage: "patchy-blatchy" and "slippery-slidy." How do these adjectives help the reader understand the scene?

Now you try it:

Write two sentences about going on a long car trip. Your first sentence should contain a strong verb that creates a vivid picture for the reader. Your second sentence should use a hyphenated adjective that either rhymes (like "patchy-blatchy") or has alliteration (like "slippery-slidy"). It's OK to make up part of the hyphenated adjective (like "blatchy"), but it must be understandable to the reader. Remember that the purpose of this kind of diction is to make an experience come alive for the reader.

Diction

Read and think:

"Swallow, Swallow, little Swallow," said the Prince, "far away across the city I see a young man in a garret*. He is leaning over a desk covered with papers, and in a tumbler by his side there is a bunch of withered violets. His hair is brown and **crisp**, and his lips are red as a pomegranate, and he has large and dreamy eyes."

Oscar Wilde, "The Happy Prince," *The Happy Prince and Other Tales*

*an attic room

Talk about it:

1. Look carefully at the diction in this passage. Is the young man rich or poor? How do you know?

2. What does it mean to have "crisp" hair? Sketch a picture of someone with "crisp" hair.

Now you try it:

Write a short description of a dog. First, decide whether you want to describe a fancy, pedigreed dog or a scruffy mutt. Then capture the dog by using strong diction. Don't explain that the dog is fancy or scruffy. Instead, use "perfect" words to create a picture of the dog for the reader. Use Wilde's passage as a model.

Diction

Read and think:

In our nation work and wealth abound. Our population grows. Commerce **crowds** our rivers and rails, our skies, harbors, and highways. Our soil is fertile, our agriculture productive. The air **rings** with the song of our industry—rolling mills and blast furnaces, dynamos, dams, and assembly lines—the chorus of **America the bountiful.**

Dwight D. Eisenhower, Second Inaugural Address, January 21, 1957

Talk about it:

1. Look at the boldfaced verbs ("crowds," "rings") in the passage. Notice how clearly you can "see" the action because of the strong verbs. How would it change the impact of the passage if we changed the verbs? For example:

   *Our rivers, rails, skies, harbors, and highways **are** busy with commerce. Our soil is fertile, our agriculture productive. The air **is** full of the sounds of work.*

2. Look at the final phrase of the passage ("America the bountiful"). What does Eisenhower's use of "bountiful" instead of, for example, "beautiful" tell us about his attitude toward America?

Now you try it:

Use the verb "crowds" in a sentence, but instead of having the word express excitement and pride, have it express a feeling of danger and possible disaster. Remember that, in many cases, the context of the word determines its deeper, connotative meaning.

Diction

Read and think:

Brown as a coffee-berry, rugged, **pistoled**, **spurred**, wary, **indefeasible***, I saw my old friend, Deputy-Marshal Buck Caperton, stumble, with jingling rowels**, into a chair in the marshal's outer office.

O. Henry, "The Lonesome Road," 41 Stories by O. Henry

*something that can't be canceled
**a sharp-toothed wheel in the end of a spur

Talk about it:

1. Look at the first two boldfaced words ("pistoled" and "spurred"). Both of these words describe Deputy-Marshal Buck Caperton. What do they mean? Explain how the meaning would change if O. Henry had written:

   I saw my old friend Deputy-Marshal Buck Caperton, who was wearing a pistol and spurs, stumble, with jingling rowels, into a chair in the marshal's outer office.

2. The word "indefeasible" is usually used to describe a contract or some kind of legal document that cannot be canceled. O. Henry uses it to describe a character. What does it mean in this context? In other words, how can a person be indefeasible? What does this choice of words add to the impact of the sentence?

Now you try it:

Write a sentence describing someone whose clothes are really wild. In your sentence use at least one noun (like "pistol") as an adjective (like "pistoled").

Diction

Read and think:

People who live in Tornado Alley know when tornadoes are likely to form. The first sign is thunderclouds building in the distance. These can be spotted by their **anvil** tops. From a distance, the clouds bulge out on top. This shows that the updrafts in the cloud are very strong, so the storm may be a powerful supercell.

Chris Oxlade, *Storm Warning: Tornadoes*

Talk about it:

1. Note that this is informational text. As such, the purpose is to pass on knowledge, to teach. Diction here is precise and unambiguous. With this in mind, look at the third sentence. The clouds are described as having "anvil tops." Sketch a picture of clouds with anvil tops.

2. How would the impact of the sentence change if we wrote it like this?

   The clouds can be spotted by their flat tops.

Now you try it:

Think about a storm in your part of the country. Write a sentence describing the clouds. Use diction that is precise and vivid so that your reader thoroughly understands what the clouds look like.

Diction

Read and think:

How well I recollect the kind of day it was! I smell the fog that hung about the place; I see the hoar frost*, ghostly, through it; I feel my rimy** hair fall clammy on my cheek; I look along the dim perspective of the schoolroom, with a **sputtering** candle here and there to light up the foggy morning, and the breath of the boys wreathing*** and smoking in the raw cold as they blow upon their fingers, and tap their feet upon the floor.

Charles Dickens, David Copperfield

*white ice crystals that form on the ground in cold weather
**covered with frost
***twisting around like a wreath

Talk about it:

1. What words help you understand that the room is cold and dark?

Words that tell you the room is cold	Words that tell you the room is dark

2. What is a "sputtering" candle? How does describing the candle help you understand the feeling of the whole room?

Now you try it:

Describe a room that is uncomfortable. In your description, use words that are clear, concrete, and exact, as Dickens does. Use a vivid adjective to describe an object in the room (like "sputtering candle"). The adjective and object should help your readers understand the feeling of the room. Remember, don't simply state that it's uncomfortable. Instead, create a picture for the reader, capturing how specific aspects of the room make it uncomfortable.

Write Your Own Diction Lessons

Now that you have studied the Diction lessons, it is time for some additional practice. One way to practice is to write your own voice lessons. These pages include quotations you can use to write your own "Talk about it" questions. **Remember that you are not writing comprehension questions.** Instead, you are writing questions that help others understand the power of language: how the author uses diction to express voice and to create a world for the reader. To help you write your questions, I have included a hint—a suggestion for focusing your questions. Please do not let the hint limit your questions. Instead, allow your creativity and understanding of the writer's craft lead you to many different places.

You can also write "Now you try it" exercises for each quotation. Remember to use the quote as a model and to design an activity that puts the craft of the quotation into practice.

When you have written questions and exercises, exchange them with other students in your class and try answering each other's questions and exercises. Or you can exchange questions and exercises with members of another class. Discuss the quotations, plan and discuss the questions, practice, and share the craft. This is the way writers learn.

1. Many mammals are at home in trees. The sharp claws and flexible legs of squirrels are adaptations for running up and down trees. They have **keen-sighted, forward-facing** eyes that allow precise judgment for leaping from branch to branch.

Robert Snedden, *Adaptation and Survival*

Hint: Focus on the precise, hyphenated adjectives.

2. My attention was first directed to the broad-tailed hummer by seeing him **darting** about in the air with the swiftness of an arrow, **sipping** honey from the flower cups, and then **flying** to the twigs of a dead tree that stood in the marsh.

Leander Sylvester Keyser, *Birds of the Rockies*

Hint: Focus on strong verbs.

3. Ah, distinctly I remember, it was in the bleak December,
And each separate dying ember wrought its ghost upon the floor.
Eagerly I wished the morrow;—vainly I had sought to borrow
From my books surcease of sorrow—sorrow for the lost Lenore—
For the rare and radiant maiden whom the angels name Lenore—
Nameless here for evermore.

And the silken sad uncertain rustling of each purple curtain
Thrilled me—filled me with **fantastic** terrors never felt before;
So that now, to still the beating of my heart, I stood repeating
"'Tis some visitor entreating entrance at my chamber door—
Some late visitor entreating entrance at my chamber door;—
This it is and nothing more."

Edgar Allan Poe, "The Raven"

Hint: Look at words used in unusual ways.

4. Mrs. Ferrars was a little, thin woman, **upright, even to formality,** in her figure, and **serious, even to sourness,** in her aspect.

Jane Austen, Sense and Sensibility

Hint: Look at words that help the reader visualize the character.

Detail

Introduction

Detail is what makes writing come alive. Detail includes facts, observations, reasons, examples, and incidents that a writer uses to develop a subject. Specific details create a clear mental picture for the reader by focusing on particulars rather than abstractions. In other words, instead of saying, "I had a great time at the party," good writers will fill their papers with the *specifics* of what made the party fun. "A great time" means different things to different people. Was the music great? The food? The company? Were there games? Was there dancing? Swimming? Was your best friend there, or did you like it because you met new and interesting people? You get the idea. Detail helps your reader get an exact picture of what you're writing about.

Detail also helps to focus the reader's attention on important ideas and shapes the reader's understanding of a topic. For example, let's say you took a trip to the beach and wanted to describe what you saw there. You can't describe everything—that would make a boring and rambling essay. Instead, you have to decide your focus. You could focus on the animals you saw at the beach (birds, crabs and other shellfish, fish); you could focus on the people you saw at the beach; you could focus on the terrible sunburn you got while you were there. Focus also includes the attitude you want to convey. Maybe your attitude is that the beach is a place of peace and relaxation, or maybe you want to express your discomfort with the heat, sand, crowds, and sunburn. You decide. And once you decide, you select the details that support, develop, and enliven your focus and attitude. If you do it like the experts, the detail you select will guide your reader into the experience in just the way you want. You get to choose how your reader "sees" your experiences!

In addition, authors depend on detail to help the reader enter the experience created by the writing. A writer can emphasize a point by focusing the reader's attention on a thought or reason through detail. For example, if you are writing a paper about pets and decide to focus on the benefits of pet ownership, you need to fill your paper with specific details about these benefits. Don't tell your reader that pets are loyal and comforting. Instead, show details of how a specific dog saved a child's life; create a picture of a lonely person being comforted by a purring cat. Detail allows the reader to participate as an equal partner in the world the writer has created and to follow the writer's ideas in the way the writer intends.

Getting Started with Detail

- Take a few minutes to practice before you begin the Detail lessons. Think of a shopping trip to your favorite mall. Think about everything you might look at in that mall.

- Now make a list of the details you might focus on during a shopping trip to the mall.

- Next, decide your focus: people, clothes, food, variety of experiences, commercialism, stores, unexpected things you find, activities, specific parts of the mall (like the food court). You decide. Write your focus below.

- Now write down your attitude. Are you thrilled, critical, neutral, mocking, angry, awed?

- Finally, list as many details as you can that support your focus and develop your attitude. Choose only details that help your reader understand the focus and attitude you want to convey.

- This time, shift your attention, and think about your favorite time of year at the mall. Your favorite time of year is the focus. Your attitude should be celebratory and happy. List all of the details you can that support this focus and attitude.

Notice how different this list is from your original list. Detail, used well, guides the experience of the reader where the writer wants him/her to go.

Think about focus and attitude as you complete the Detail lessons that follow. Pay careful attention to how accomplished writers use concrete, specific details. With practice, you can learn to use detail to shape your reader's understanding.

Detail

Read and think:

On a flat road runs the well-train'd runner,
He is lean and sinewy with muscular legs,
He is thinly clothed, he leans forward as he runs,
With lightly closed fists and arms partially rais'd.

Walt Whitman, "The Runner," *Leaves of Grass*

Talk about it:

1. Whitman focuses on the "well-train'd runner" himself—not a race or his speed or an audience. Underline the details that focus your attention on the runner and talk about their effectiveness.

2. Select a detail from the poem that captures a positive quality of the runner. Can you change the positive quality to a negative quality by changing the detail?

Now you try it:

Write a paragraph using details to give the reader a picture of an athlete you admire. Don't explain why you admire the athlete. Instead, use details to show the admirable qualities of the athlete. If you want to experiment, try writing a poem, like Whitman's, instead of a paragraph.

Detail

Read and think:

The rapidly expanding world population is a major pressure on water availability. In countries such as Pakistan and Nigeria, populations are expected to triple by 2050. Not only do more people need more water, but the amount of water people use has doubled in the last 30 years. Rates of usage are still increasing. When standards of living increase, more people across the world benefit from improved sanitation. They start to rely on washing machines, showers, baths, and flushing toilets. The amount of water used per person increases dramatically.

Richard Spilsbury, *Managing Water*

Talk about it:

1. What is the focus or main idea of this paragraph? What details support and strengthen the main idea?

2. How would the impact of this paragraph change if it were written like this? Think about it in terms of the level of detail provided in the original versus the generic text below.

World population affects water availability. The population in lots of countries is growing. There are more people, and these people are starting to use more water. Improved sanitation requires more water.

Now you try it:

In the space below, write three sentences that provide detailed support for the main idea of a paragraph. Your paragraph should start with the sentence below and be clearly developed like Spilsbury's paragraph.

There are many different kinds of animals that live in the ocean.

Detail

Read and think:

Just at daybreak, I was awakened by a series of awful screams from Bill. They weren't yells, or howls, or shouts, or whoops, or yawps, such as you'd expect from a manly set of vocal organs—they were simply indecent, terrifying, humiliating screams, such as women emit when they see ghosts or caterpillars. It's an awful thing to hear a strong, desperate, fat man scream incontinently in a cave at daybreak.

O. Henry, "The Ransom of Red Chief"

Talk about it:

1. What is the main idea (topic sentence) or focus of this paragraph? State it as simply as you can. How do the details in this paragraph make the main idea come alive?

2. What effect do the details in the description of the man in the last sentence ("a strong, desperate, fat man") have on the meaning of the paragraph?

Now you try it:

Write a simple topic sentence that describes an incident that you remember very well. Then list all of the details you can think of that would help someone else understand what happened. Share your sentence and list with a partner. After your partner has read your sentence and list, have him/her explain to you why your memory of this incident is so vivid. If your list is full of concrete details, your partner should be able to do this easily.

Detail

Read and think:

So, first of all, let me assert my firm belief that the only thing we have to fear is fear itself—nameless, unreasoning, unjustified terror which paralyzes needed efforts to convert retreat into advance.

Franklin D. Roosevelt, First Inaugural Address, March 4, 1933

Talk about it:

1. The focus of Roosevelt's sentence is on fear. Discuss the details in the sentence that help you understand exactly what he means by fear.

2. How would the feeling and impact of this passage change if Roosevelt had written it like this?

   First, let me tell you that fear itself is the only thing we really need to fear.

Now you try it:

Complete the following sentence with details that help your reader know exactly what you mean. Use Roosevelt's sentence as a model.

Let me assert my firm belief that a happy life must include friends—

Detail

Read and think:

I found employment, the third day after my arrival, in stowing a sloop* with a load of oil. It was new, dirty, and hard work for me; but I went at it with a glad heart and a willing hand. I was now my own master. It was a happy moment, the rapture of which can be understood only by those who have been slaves. It was the first work, the reward of which was to be entirely my own. There was no Master Hugh standing ready, the moment I earned the money, to rob me of it. I worked that day with a pleasure I had never before experienced. I was at work for myself and newly-married wife. It was to me the starting-point of a new existence.

Frederick Douglass, *Narrative of the Life of Frederick Douglass, An American Slave*

*a sailing boat

Talk about it:

1. The first sentence of the passage is a general statement, stating that Douglass, newly escaped from slavery, has a job. The rest of the paragraph uses details to help the reader understand the nature and importance of this job. What details do you remember most about this paragraph? Why do you think that is so?

2. Underline the details that help the reader understand Douglass happiness. What effect do these details have on the reader?

Now you try it:

Write a paragraph that starts with the following sentence: *I went to a football game Friday evening.* Then use detail to capture the aspects of the game you liked. Don't explain why you liked the game. Instead, bring the reader into the experience of the game through carefully chosen detail.

Detail

Read and think:

As I was waiting, a man came out of a side room, and at a glance I was sure he must be Long John. His left leg was cut off close by the hip, and under the left shoulder he carried a crutch, which he managed with wonderful dexterity, hopping about upon it like a bird. He was very tall and strong, with a face as big as a ham—plain and pale, but intelligent and smiling. Indeed, he seemed in the most cheerful spirits, whistling as he moved about among the tables, with a merry word or a slap on the shoulder for the more favoured of his guests.

Robert Louis Stevenson, *Treasure Island*

Talk about it:

1. Look at the following rewriting of the second sentence in the paragraph:

   He was missing a leg and walked with a crutch, which he used well.

   Which sentence is more alive and engrossing? Which one brings you into the scene? Why?

2. Sketch a little picture of Long John. What details are in your sketch? Why are they memorable?

Now you try it:

Rewrite Stevenson's sentence below, replacing all of the underlined words with words of your own. Your sentence should describe a mean neighbor.

He was very <u>tall</u> and <u>strong</u>, with a face as <u>big</u> as a <u>ham</u>—<u>plain</u> and <u>pale</u>, but <u>intelligent</u> and <u>smiling</u>.

Detail

Read and think:

If you shut your eyes and are a lucky one, you may see at times a shapeless pool of lovely pale colours suspended in the darkness; then if you squeeze your eyes tighter, the pool begins to take shape, and the colours become so vivid that with another squeeze they must go on fire. But just before they go on fire you see the lagoon. This is the nearest you ever get to it on the mainland, just one heavenly moment; if there could be two moments you might see the surf and hear the mermaids singing.

J. M. Barrie, *Peter Pan*

Talk about it:

1. Think of one word of your choice to describe the lagoon. Which details in the passage support your word choice?

2. The narrator in this passage talks directly to the reader. Which details help the reader to fully participate in the scene?

Now you try it:

Rewrite Barrie's description eliminating all of the specific detail. Discuss the change in impact and meaning.

Detail | **33**

Detail

Read and think:

More than half of the day was far from enjoyable. The morning was magnificent, but the light too dazzling, the sun too fierce. As soon as I got out I felt as if I should drop off the horse. My large handkerchief kept the sun from my neck, but the fierce heat caused soul and sense, brain and eye, to reel. I never saw or felt the like of it. I was at a height of 12,000 feet, where, of course, the air was highly rarefied*, and the snow was so pure and dazzling that I was obliged to keep my eyes shut as much as possible to avoid snow blindness. The sky was a different and terribly fierce color; and when I caught a glimpse of the sun, he was white and unwinking… I suffered so from nausea, exhaustion, and pains from head to foot, that I felt as if I must lie down in the snow. It may have been partly the early stage of soroche, or mountain sickness.

Isabella L. Bird, *A Lady's Life in the Rocky Mountains*

*thin, containing little oxygen

Talk about it:

1. As Bird begins the description of this day, she says, "More than half of the day was far from enjoyable." Which details support this statement? Fill in the chart below with details.

the air	the snow	the sky	her physical condition

2. Why do you think Bird describes the discomfort of the mountains and does not mention the beauty of the scene?

Now you try it:

Write two sentences to describe a splendid day. Don't explain, but give details to make the day come alive for the reader. Your details should focus on the weather and your physical condition. Use Bird's paragraph as a model.

Detail

Read and think:

Even in the days before my teacher came, I used to feel along the square stiff boxwood hedges, and, guided by the sense of smell, would find the first violets and lilies. There, too, after a fit of temper, I went to find comfort and to hide my hot face in the cool leaves and grass. What joy it was to lose myself in that garden of flowers, to wander happily from spot to spot, until, coming suddenly upon a beautiful vine, I recognized it by its leaves and blossoms, and knew it was the vine which covered the tumble-down summer-house at the farther end of the garden!

Helen Keller, The Story of My Life

Talk about it:

1. Helen Keller contracted an illness when she was 19 months old that left her blind and deaf. She eventually had a brilliant teacher who taught her to read, write, and speak— experiences that are described in her autobiography. Do the experiences described in this paragraph happen before or after Keller learns to read, write, and speak? How do you know? Focus on detail.

2. How would the impact of Keller's paragraph change if it were written like this?

   Before I learned to read, write, and speak, life was hard. I had a bad temper and needed a lot of comfort. I used to go in the garden and feel my way around. Sometimes that made me happy.

Now you try it:

Write a paragraph about a place you have gone to find comfort. Based on Keller's paragraph, use the following sentence frame as a guide.

When I was feeling sad, I went to _____. How comforting it was

to _____ !

Detail

Read and think:

Sherlock Holmes took the lamp and led the way, for Thaddeus Sholto's teeth were chattering in his head. So shaken was he that I had to pass my hand under his arm as we went up the stairs, for his knees were trembling under him. Twice as we ascended Holmes whipped his lens out of his pocket and carefully examined marks which appeared to me to be mere shapeless smudges of dust upon the cocoa-nut matting which served as a stair-carpet. He walked slowly from step to step, holding the lamp, and shooting keen glances to right and left.

Sir Arthur Conan Doyle, *The Sign of the Four*

Talk about it:

1. What kind of a man is Sherlock Holmes? Which details in this paragraph reveal his character?

2. How would it change the impact of the paragraph if we changed the paragraph to this?

   Sherlock Holmes led the way upstairs. He walked slowly and looked carefully at everything.

Now you try it:

Write a paragraph describing someone you admire. Don't explain why you think the person is admirable. Instead, use vivid detail to capture the person's actions. These actions should reveal the person's admirable qualities. Use Doyle's paragraph as a model.

Write Your Own Detail Lessons

Now that you have studied the Detail lessons, it is time for some additional practice. One way to practice is to write your own voice lessons. These pages include quotations you can use to write your own "Talk about it" questions. **Remember that you are not writing comprehension questions.** Instead, you are writing questions that help others understand the power of language: how the author uses detail to express voice and to create a world for the reader. To help you write your questions, I have included a hint—a suggestion for focusing your questions. Please do not let the hint limit your questions. Instead, allow your creativity and understanding of the writer's craft lead you to many different places.

You can also write "Now you try it" exercises for each quotation. Remember to use the quote as a model and to design an activity that puts the craft of the quotation into practice.

When you have written questions and exercises, exchange them with other students in your class and try answering each other's questions and exercises. Or you can exchange questions and exercises with members of another class. Discuss the quotations, plan and discuss the questions, practice, and share the craft. This is the way writers learn.

1. We love all the seasons; the snows and bare woods of winter; the rush of growing things and the blossom-spray of spring; the yellow grain, the ripening fruits and tasseled corn, and the deep, leafy shades that are heralded by "the green dance of summer"; and the sharp fall winds that tear the brilliant banners with which the trees greet the dying year.

Theodore Roosevelt, *An Autobiography*

Hint: Think about how detail helps the reader understand the opening statement.

2. In one particular way, cars have always been friendly to the environment. Most of the materials in them have always been recycled. A car or other vehicle contains large amounts of steel, some aluminum, lead, and other valuable metals. All these metals can be separated from each other, melted down, and used again. There is a huge worldwide industry involved in breaking up damaged vehicles and separating the different metals in them for recycling.

Andrew Solway, *The Impact of Environmentalism: Transportation*

Hint: Think about how the detail explains and supports the main idea.

3. One man who knew Lincoln at New Salem, says the first time he saw him he was lying on a trundle-bed covered with books and papers and rocking a cradle with his foot.

Alexander K. McClure, *Lincoln's Yarns and Stories*

Hint: Think about what the details reveal about Abraham Lincoln.

4. My back had now become very stiff and sore, my tonsils were painful from the cabman's fingers, and the skin of my neck had been scratched by his nails; my feet hurt exceedingly and I was lame from a little cut on one foot.

H. G. Wells, *The Invisible Man*

Hint: Focus on how the detail makes the general focus (being hurt) come alive.

Figurative Language 1:
Metaphor, Simile, and Personification

Introduction

Metaphors, similes, and personification belong to a class of language called **figurative language.** Figurative language is any language that is *not* used in a literal (meaning exactly what it says) way. It's a way of saying one thing and meaning another. We use figurative language, or **figures of speech,** all of the time in spoken English. When we go to a baseball game, for example, we might make comments like these:

- That pitcher doctored the ball!
- The ball sat in the outfield.
- Jimmy ran like lightning to first base.

If we look at these statements literally, they make no sense at all. A pitcher is not a doctor. A ball can't "sit." Jimmy is not "lightning" and can't run at the speed of light. Even though the statements make no literal sense at all, we understand them completely. That's because we've been speaking figurative language all of our lives! When someone says the "pitcher doctored the ball," we know what it means: The pitcher cheated in some way when he threw the ball. When someone says the ball "sat" in the outfield, we don't have to try to picture the ball with legs, sitting down on a chair in a field. We know what it means: that no one was quick to get the ball. And no one thinks that Jimmy turned into a flash of lightning. We know that Jimmy is a fast runner—the fastest—like lightning.

Why do we use figurative language? We use figurative language because it's a rich, strong, and vivid way to express meaning. By using figurative language, we are able to say much more in fewer words. When Robert Burns, a famous poet, says, "O my Luve's [Love is] like a red, red rose," he is saying many things: his love is beautiful, soft, and fragrant. The rose is red, the color of passion and love. This adds another dimension. The rose also has thorns, which says that there's a potential danger in loving her. She may hurt him. By comparing his love to a red rose, the poet is able to compress or squeeze many ideas into a single line.

Figurative language is useful, but it can be overdone too. When a figure of speech is used over and over again, it loses its freshness and originality and becomes a cliché, a stale and overused expression. Here are some examples of figures of speech that have become clichés:

- pretty as a picture
- quiet as a mouse
- Laughter is the best medicine.
- Every cloud has a silver lining.
- It happened in the dead of night.

There are many more. These overused figures of speech no longer get the reader's attention. As you learn to understand and write figurative language like a pro, search for figures of speech that you haven't heard a million times (that's figurative!) before. You will get better with practice.

As you probably understand by now, there are several different kinds of figurative language. In this section we will explore three of the most important figures of speech: metaphor, simile, and personification.

Metaphor and Simile

Metaphors and similes are used to compare things that are not usually seen as similar. Metaphors **imply** the comparison, and similes **state** the comparison directly. Suppose, for example, you've just taken an extremely hard test. To make this idea into a **metaphor**, you could say, "That test was a bear!" You are not saying that it was a literal bear but that it was unpredictable and hard to deal with. The comparison between the test and a bear is not directly stated. Instead, the comparison is implied or suggested. You identify the bear with the test. That's what a metaphor does. A metaphor implies a comparison in order to bring fresh, rich meaning to writing (and speaking).

A **simile** is a comparison too. With a simile, however, the comparison is directly stated. To make the "test" metaphor into a simile, you make the comparison explicit: "That test was like struggling with a bear!" It is still nonliteral language—taking the test is not really like struggling with a bear—but with a simile you come right out and state the comparison. Similes have signal words that give you a hint a simile is coming. These words include "as," "like," "than," "similar to," and "resembles." Be careful though. These words don't always indicate similes. If I say, "I look like my sister," I am not using a simile. It's a literal statement; I *do* look like my sister. To be a simile or a metaphor, the comparison must be of essentially unlike things.

Metaphors and similes have **literal terms** and **figurative terms.**

- The **literal** term is what we are comparing to something else. It's what's real; it means what it is. For example, the literal term in the metaphor "That test was a bear!" is "test." We are really talking about a test.

- The **figurative** term is what is being compared to the literal term. The figurative term means something other than itself, something nonliteral. The figurative term in the metaphor is "bear." The test is not a bear, but it has some bear-like qualities that can help us understand just how hard the test was.

Fill out the following chart to practice these concepts:

Figure of speech	Metaphor or simile?	Literal term	Figurative term
I got a flood of mail yesterday.			
Alice sang like a crow.			
Jeff grew like a weed over the summer.			
The shoes cost a king's ransom.			

Personification

Another popular figure of speech is **personification**. Personification is a special kind of metaphor that gives human qualities to something that is not human, such as an animal, an object, or an idea. For example, if we say, "The tree sighed sadly in the cold," we are using personification. A tree can't really sigh or be sad. We are giving the tree characteristics of a person. Personification, since it is a kind of metaphor, has a literal and figurative term. In this example, the literal term is the tree (it really is a tree), and the figurative term is a person (the tree is not really a person who can sigh and be sad). In personification the figurative term is always a person.

Getting Started with Metaphor, Simile, and Personification

Practice writing examples of metaphor, simile, and personification for the literal terms below. The first one is done for you as an example.

Literal term	Possible figurative terms	Metaphor	Simile	Personification
friendship	lighthouse warm blanket	Donna's friendship is a lighthouse.	Donna's friendship is like a lighthouse.	Donna's friendship wrapped my sadness in a warm blanket.
football game				
cleaning your room				
shirt				
cafeteria lunch				

As you learn about the power of metaphor, simile, and personification in the following lessons, pay particular attention to how fresh and original the figures of speech are in the hands of expert writers. With practice, you can learn to write expert metaphors, similes, and personification yourself.

Metaphor, Simile, and Personification

Read and think:

It is a dreary ride of thirty miles over the low brown plains to Denver, very little settled, and with trails going in all directions. My sailing orders were "steer south, and keep to the best beaten track," and it seemed like embarking on the ocean without a compass. The rolling brown waves on which you see a horse a mile and a half off impress one strangely, and at noon the sky darkened up for another storm, the mountains swept down in blackness to the Plains, and the higher peaks took on a ghastly grimness horrid to behold.

Isabella L. Bird, *A Lady's Life in the Rocky Mountains*

Talk about it:

1. Identify two examples of figurative language in the passage. Are the figures of speech metaphors or similes? How do you know the language is figurative?

Figure of speech	Metaphor or simile?	How you know

2. What does the figurative language add to the passage?

Now you try it:

Rewrite the passage from Bird's description *without* any figurative language. Contrast your sentences with the original. Talk about the differences with a partner.

Metaphor, Simile, and Personification

Read and think:

And dark in the dark old inn-yard a stable-wicket creaked
Where Tim the ostler* listened; his face was white and peaked;
His eyes were hollows of madness, his hair like mouldy hay,
But he loved the landlord's daughter,
The landlord's red-lipped daughter,
Dumb as a dog he listened, and he heard the robber say—

Alfred Noyes, "The Highwayman"

*someone who takes care of horses

Talk about it:

1. Identify the metaphor in this stanza from "The Highwayman." What is the literal term?
   What is the figurative term? What does the metaphor mean?

2. There are two similes in this stanza (lines 3 and 6). Identify the similes and the figurative
   and literal terms. Explain the second simile.

Now you try it:

Rewrite the figurative term from the metaphor in line 3. Your new metaphor should make
Tim the ostler seem silly and happy. Remember, don't describe his eyes. Capture them with
a metaphor.

His eyes were _____

Metaphor, Simile, and Personification

Read and think:

Fourscore and seven years ago our fathers brought forth upon this continent a new nation, conceived in liberty, and dedicated to the proposition that all men are created equal.

Abraham Lincoln, The Gettysburg Address

Talk about it:

1. There is an implied metaphor in these famous lines from The Gettysburg Address. What two essentially unlike things are being compared?

2. Identify the figurative and literal terms (even if they are not directly stated) in the metaphor.

Now you try it:

Rewrite Lincoln's sentence leaving out all of the figurative language. Discuss how the elimination of figurative language changes the power of the sentence.

Metaphor, Simile, and Personification

Read and think:

The Time Traveller put his hand to his head. He spoke like one who was trying to keep hold of an idea that eluded him.

H. G. Wells, *The Time Machine*

Talk about it:

1. Look at the second sentence. Is "like one who was trying to keep hold of an idea that eluded him" a simile? Explain.

2. How would you act out these two sentences? Get in groups and plan a little performance of the two sentences. See which group can act it out the best. Would figurative language help you act out the sentences?

Now you try it:

Take the second sentence above and use a simile to clarify how the Time Traveller spoke. Use the following sentence frame. Then fill in the chart. Remember that a simile compares things that are not usually seen as similar.

He spoke like _____.

Literal term	Figurative term

Metaphor, Simile, and Personification

Read and think:

All the world's a stage,
And all the men and women merely players:
They have their exits and their entrances;
And one man in his time plays many parts,

William Shakespeare, *As You Like It*, Act II, scene 7

Talk about it:

1. These famous lines from *As You Like It* contain an extended metaphor, a metaphor that continues over several lines and is developed in several ways. There are two closely connected literal terms: "all the world" and the people in the world ("all the men and women"). What are the figurative terms that go with these two literal terms?

2. How do lines three and four extend the metaphor and make it more interesting?

Now you try it:

Write an extended metaphor like Shakespeare's. Compare the world to something else:

All the world's a _____. Then extend your metaphor, developing your figurative term with a related metaphor about the people in the world. Use Shakespeare's lines as a model, but you don't have to write your lines in blank verse.

Metaphor, Simile, and Personification

Read and think:

A cell's DNA can be thought of as an instruction manual—a set of instructions for making parts of a cell. Each gene is the plan for a specific part. The parts that genes carry instructions for are called proteins. If the instruction written in a gene is activated, a protein is created.

Robert Snedden, *DNA and Genetic Engineering*

Talk about it:

1. Notice that informational text uses figurative language too. It is often used to explain the unfamiliar by comparing it to something familiar. In this quotation, is the sentence "A cell's DNA can be thought of as an instruction manual—a set of instructions for making parts of a cell" a metaphor or a simile? Explain your thinking.

2. What are the literal and figurative terms? How does Snedden extend the figure of speech?

Now you try it:

Write one sentence that describes a park. First describe it literally (how the park really is). Then support your description with a simile. Use this pattern for your sentence:

The park _____, like _____.

Metaphor, Simile, and Personification

Read and think:

Thirty-four years ago, the man whose life we celebrate today spoke to us down there, at the other end of this Mall, in words that moved the conscience of a nation. Like a prophet of old, he told of his dream that one day America would rise up and treat all its citizens as equals before the law and in the heart. Martin Luther King's dream was the American Dream.

William Jefferson Clinton, Second Inaugural Address, January 20, 1993

Talk about it:

1. Find the simile in the passage and identify the literal and figurative terms.

2. How is the meaning of the passage deepened by the simile?

Now you try it:

Write a sentence like President Clinton's second sentence. Write the sentence about a teacher or a coach you admire. Your sentence should contain an original simile. Use Clinton's speech as a model.

Metaphor, Simile, and Personification

Read and think:

Clara [impulsively]: How do you do? [She sits down on the ottoman beside Eliza, devouring her with her eyes].

George Bernard Shaw, *Pygmalion*, Act 3

Talk about it:

1. This quote is from a play. Clara has just met Eliza (one of the main characters) for the first time. The words in brackets are the stage directions. There is an implied metaphor in the stage directions. What are the literal and figurative terms of the metaphor? In other words, what two things are being compared?

2. Why doesn't Shaw simply say, "She sits down beside Eliza and looks closely at her"?

Now you try it:

Write a sentence with an implied metaphor. Your topic is a group of people trying to get into a store that is having a huge sale. Capture how they behave with your implied metaphor. Don't state the metaphor. (For example, "They were wild animals as they waited to get in the store.") Instead, let their actions imply your metaphor. Use Shaw's stage directions as a model.

Metaphor, Simile, and Personification

Read and think:

The ruddy brick floor smiled up at the smoky ceiling; the oaken settles*, shiny with long wear, exchanged cheerful glances with each other; plates on the dresser grinned at pots on the shelf, and the merry firelight flickered and played over everything without distinction.

Kenneth Grahame, *The Wind in the Willows*

*long, wooden benches with high backs that usually have storage space in the seat

Talk about it:

1. Remember that personification is a kind of metaphor, an implied comparison that always has a human being as its figurative term. Identify the examples of personification in the passage, and fill in the following chart:

Example of personification	Literal term	Figurative term (What are the person's characteristics?)

2. How does the use of personification help the reader visualize and connect to the passage? What feeling is created by the personification?

Now you try it:

Write a short paragraph describing a friend's room. In your description, use personification at least one time. Use Grahame's paragraph as a model.

Metaphor, Simile, and Personification

Read and think:

And now the Storm-blast came, and he

Was tyrannous and strong:

He struck with his o'ertaking wings,

And chased us south along.

Samuel Taylor Coleridge, "The Rime of the Ancient Mariner"

Talk about it:

1. Underline the example of personification in the first two lines. What are the literal and figurative terms?

2. Is the third line an example of personification? Defend your ideas.

Now you try it:

Describe a storm or an exceptionally beautiful day. In your description, use at least one example of personification. Your description can be poetry or prose. Exchange your description with a partner and have your partner identify your literal and figurative term.

Write Your Own Figurative Language Lessons on Metaphor, Simile, and Personification

Now that you have studied the Figurative Language lessons on metaphors, similes, and personification, it is time for some additional practice. One way to practice is to write your own voice lessons. These pages include quotations you can use to write your own "Talk about it" questions. **Remember that you are not writing comprehension questions.** Instead, you are writing questions that help others understand the power of language: how the author uses metaphor, simile, and personification to express voice and to create a world for the reader. To help you write your questions, I have included a hint—a suggestion for focusing your questions. Please do not let the hint limit your questions. Instead, allow your creativity and understanding of the writer's craft lead you to many different places.

You can also write "Now you try it" exercises for each quotation. Remember to use the quote as a model and to design an activity that puts the craft of the quotation into practice.

When you have written questions and exercises, exchange them with other students in your class and try answering each other's questions and exercises. Or you can exchange questions and exercises with members of another class. Discuss the quotations, plan and discuss the questions, practice, and share the craft. This is the way writers learn.

1. So Eppie was reared without punishment, the burden of her misdeeds being borne vicariously by father Silas. The stone hut was made a soft nest for her, lined with downy patience; and also in the world that lay beyond the stone hut she knew nothing of frowns and denials.

   George Eliot, Silas Marner, The Weaver of Raveloe

   Hint: Look at the metaphor in this one, especially the idea of an implied metaphor.

2. Driving snow, a wind that cut like a white-hot knife, and darkness had forced them to grope for a camping place.

   Jack London, The Call of the Wild

   Hint: Focus on the simile and what it adds to the reader's understanding.

3. ...he [Martin Luther King] told of his dream that one day America would rise up and treat all its citizens as equals before the law and in the heart.

   William Jefferson Clinton, Second Inaugural Address, January 20, 1993

   Hint: Think about what personification adds to the passage.

4. With his body hunched forward and his arms stretched out straight in front of him, resting on a long, narrow set of handlebars, Obree looked like Superman flying through the air as he flew around the oval track.

Lori Hile, *Getting Ahead: Drugs, Technology, and Competitive Advantage*

Hint: Focus on the simile and how it helps the reader visualize this rider's position on a racing bicycle.

Figurative Language 2: Hyperbole, Symbol, and Irony

Introduction

This section will examine three additional kinds of figurative language: hyperbole, symbol, and irony. These figures of speech are not comparisons like metaphor, simile, and personification. However, they are similar to metaphor, simile, and personification in that they are nonliteral language: Their meaning goes beyond what is actually said. And—like metaphor, simile, and personification—hyperbole, symbol, and irony add richness and multiple meanings to writing and speech.

A **hyperbole** (pronounced *hi per´ bo lee*) is an exaggeration that is based on truth. The key to hyperboles is the part about truth. Hyperboles must be founded on truth to be meaningful. If I say, "I'm so tired I could sleep for a week," I am using hyperbole. I'm not in a coma, and I couldn't really sleep for a week, but it feels that way. The truth lies in the extent of the tiredness. It's an exaggeration, but it's based on truth. Hyperboles add interest, sometimes humor, and emphasis to what you're trying to say. Practice writing hyperboles by finishing the following sentences. Remember that your hyperbole must be an exaggeration and not literally true.

Sentence stem	Hyperbole
I was hungry enough...	
My head was...	
I laughed until...	
She ran so fast...	
When he lifted the package,...	

A **symbol** is an object or word that stands for something else—usually a complex, abstract idea. Unlike metaphors and similes, symbols do not get their meaning through comparison. Instead, they derive meaning through association, often historical, of a concrete object or word with an idea. For example, there is nothing intrinsically romantic about the human heart; but throughout history it has been associated with love in literature and art. It has thus come to symbolize love through continued association.

Like metaphors and similes, symbols have more than a literal meaning. A symbol, however, often means itself *and* something else. In other words, symbols can actually appear in the text, but they also represent an idea or abstraction. The meaning can be both literal and figurative. For example, a rainbow is a symbol of hope. If we were reading a story about a group of kids who survive a shipwreck by floating through dangerous waters on a raft, and the story ends with a description of a rainbow over an island in the distance, we would know that the kids will make it to the island. The rainbow lets us know that there is hope for these kids' futures. It *is* a rainbow, but it is *also* the symbol of hope. That is one difference between a symbol and a metaphor or simile. In a metaphor or simile, the figurative term is only something else. We can say, "Her face lit up like a billboard," but it's never a literal billboard.

Her face never becomes a billboard, of course. With symbols, however, you have the actual rainbow (or whatever the object is that has the figurative meaning) and its deeper, or associated, meaning.

Symbols, however, can also be metaphoric. When Robert Burns writes, "O my Luve's [Love is] like a red, red rose," he is using a simile. However, the rose has also become a symbol of love and beauty through historical repetition and association. So the symbol is the rose and the simile is the comparison between his love and a red rose. The key to symbols is the associated idea that underlies them. Like all figures of speech, symbols add substance and depth to writing.

Think of some symbols you are familiar with and fill in the following chart. There are some examples given to start you off.

Symbol	What the symbol stands for
lion	courage, nobility
skull and crossbones	danger, piracy

Irony is the use of language to establish a contrast between what is actually said and what is intended or meant. Irony is figurative because the language is not literal: The surface and underlying meanings are not the same. There are two basic kinds of irony: verbal and situational. With **verbal irony**, what is stated is the opposite of what is meant. We use **verbal irony** all of the time in speech. When the cafeteria has just served a tasteless and overcooked meal and you say, "Great lunch," you are using verbal irony. You are saying one thing and meaning the opposite. Like all figures of speech, verbal irony should not be taken literally.

A special case of verbal irony is **sarcasm**. **Sarcasm** is irony that is meant to mock or hurt. For example, if it's storming outside and you want to go for a swim, you might say, "Nice day, isn't it?" That is ironic but not sarcastic. It isn't a nice day, but your statement doesn't hurt anyone. If, however, someone in your class just got a terrible grade on an oral presentation and you say, "Nice job," you are being both ironic and sarcastic. It wasn't a nice job, and your comment is intended to hurt. Sarcasm is always ironic, but irony is not always sarcastic.

Situational irony exists in the context of a narrative. It occurs when events end up in a very different way than what was expected. Here is an example: *A high school junior named Linda is certain she is going to the prom, a month away, with her boyfriend. She is so certain that she has already bought her dress and made an appointment to have her hair done. In school one day, Linda makes fun of a classmate, Sarah, who does not have a date for the prom. Of course Sarah is hurt, but she just walks away. Two days before the prom, Linda learns that her boyfriend is taking Sarah to the prom, not her. Linda has no date to the prom after all.* This is situational irony. Linda makes fun of Sarah for not having a date for the prom, but it turns out that she, not Sarah, has no date for the prom. It turns out very different from what was expected.

Irony is sometimes hard to understand. It can be funny or serious, affectionate or contemptuous. You have to read carefully and watch the way the words and details are used. If you misunderstand the irony, you can miss the whole point of what you are reading. Practice will help you understand when something is ironic or not. Look at the following sentences and decide whether or not they are ironic. Place a check in the appropriate column.

Sentence	Ironic (figurative)	Not ironic (literal)
Your favorite team just lost by a wide margin and you are pretty disgusted about it. You say, "Great game!"		
You are traveling in the mountains and see a lovely meadow full of flowers. You say, "Nice view!"		
Your best friend is learning to ride a dirt bike, something you have always wanted to do. You say, "I wish I could do that!"		
Your best friend has to take care of his/her baby sister every day after school, a job you wouldn't want and your friend isn't very happy about. You say, "I wish I could do that!"		
You feel very strongly that teachers in your school give too much homework. You say, "I love doing four hours of homework every day."		

The lessons in this section will help you understand hyperboles, symbols, and irony. See how well you can use these figures of speech in your own writing.

Hyperbole, Symbol, and Irony

Read and think:

"Well!" thought Alice to herself, "after such a fall as this, I shall think nothing of tumbling down stairs! How brave they'll all think me at home! Why, I wouldn't say anything about it, even if I fell off the top of the house!"

Lewis Carroll, Alice's Adventures in Wonderland

Talk about it:

1. This is Alice's reaction after she tumbles down a long rabbit hole and starts her adventure. This is an example of a **hyperbole**, an exaggeration that is based on truth but carries the truth to such an extreme that it is no longer literally true. Of course, Alice wouldn't be as brave as she says if she fell off the top of the house. What, then, is the purpose of saying that she "wouldn't say anything about it"?

2. Compare Carroll's passage with this passage:

   After I fell down the rabbit hole, I would be very brave about falling down again. I don't think I'd be scared at all.

   Which sentence better helps the reader understand what Alice is thinking? Why?

Now you try it:

Write a sentence about a great basketball player, using a hyperbole. Model your sentence on Carroll's sentences.

Hyperbole, Symbol, and Irony

Read and think:

There are only two kinds of people who are really fascinating—people who know absolutely everything, and people who know absolutely nothing.

Oscar Wilde, The Picture of Dorian Gray

Talk about it:

1. What is the hyperbole in this sentence? What is being exaggerated?

2. What is the truth that underlies this hyperbole?

Now you try it:

Write a sentence that starts out like this:

There are only two kinds of friends that are really....

Then extend the sentence by using examples that are also examples of hyperbole. Use Wilde's sentence as a model.

Hyperbole, Symbol, and Irony

Read and think:

As fair art thou, my bonnie lass*,
So deep in luve** am I:
And I will luve thee still, my dear,
Till a' the seas gang*** dry.

Robert Burns, "A Red, Red Rose"

*pretty girl
**love
***go

Talk about it:

1. Underline the hyperbole in this poem. Which part of the hyperbole is figurative?

2. What is the speaker's attitude toward his "bonnie lass"? How does the hyperbole in this stanza help you understand his attitude?

Now you try it:

Write a four-line poem that uses a hyperbole to express a strong feeling about something you would love to own. Name the item, and use Burns' poem as a model.

Hyperbole, Symbol, and Irony

Read and think:

Tom appeared on the sidewalk with a bucket of whitewash and a long-handled brush. He surveyed the fence, and all gladness left him and a deep melancholy settled down upon his spirit. Thirty yards of board fence nine feet high. Life to him seemed hollow, and existence but a burden. Sighing, he dipped his brush and passed it along the topmost plank; repeated the operation; did it again; compared the insignificant whitewashed streak with the far-reaching continent of unwhitewashed fence, and sat down on a tree-box discouraged.

Mark Twain, *The Adventures of Tom Sawyer*

Talk about it:

1. As a punishment, Tom is told to paint a fence. He clearly does not like the task. Is the sentence, "Life to him seemed hollow, and existence but a burden," a hyperbole? Explain.

2. Find the hyperbole in the last sentence. What is the figurative term and what does it tell the reader about Tom's attitude toward the task?

Now you try it:

Write three sentences that capture your attitude toward doing homework. Use at least one hyperbole in your description.

Hyperbole, Symbol, and Irony

Read and think:

King Henry: Uneasy lies the head that wears a crown.

William Shakespeare, *Henry IV, Part II*, Act III, scene 1

Talk about it:

1. In this brief line from *Henry IV, Part II*, King Henry is talking about how difficult it is for a king to comfortably rest. He does this by invoking a symbol: the crown. Remember that a symbol is itself *and* something else. The crown is a literal crown, but it also means something else. What is the "something else"? When you identify the "something else," you have understood the symbol.

2. How would the impact of this line change if Shakespeare had written it like this?

Ah, a king does not rest easily.

Now you try it:

The crown is a traditional symbol, one that has been used in literature throughout much of written history. A traditional symbol brings with it a consistent, deep meaning in a specific culture. Fill in the following chart with as many traditional symbols as you can think of. Combine your chart with others in the class to make a class chart of traditional symbols that have consistent meaning in our culture.

Symbol	What the symbol stands for

Hyperbole, Symbol, and Irony

Read and think:

And the rocket's red glare, the bombs bursting in air,
Gave proof through the night that our flag was still there;
Oh, say, does that star-spangled banner yet wave
O'er the land of the free and the home of the brave?

Francis Scott Key, "The Star-Spangled Banner"

Talk about it:

1. What does the flag symbolize? How does calling the flag the "star-spangled banner" deepen our understanding of the symbolic value of the flag?

2. Is "the rocket's red glare" a symbol? Explain your answer thoroughly.

Now you try it:

The dove has become a traditional symbol of peace. Write a few sentences in which you use a dove to symbolize the promise of peace after a period of great turmoil. Your sentences should describe both the turmoil and the coming of the dove.

Hyperbole, Symbol, and Irony

Read and think:

And therefore I am come amongst you at this time, not as for my recreation or disport*, but being resolved, in the midst and heat of the battle, to live or die amongst you all; to lay down, for my God, and for my kingdom, and for my people, my honor and my blood, even the dust.

Queen Elizabeth I, Speech to the Troops at Tilbury, 1588

*sport

Talk about it:

1. Blood (line 4) is a symbol in this quotation from a rallying speech by Queen Elizabeth I to her troops as they go into battle. It is blood, but it is also something else. What is the something else?

2. How does the use of a symbol help you understand Elizabeth's attitude toward her troops and her country?

Now you try it:

Write a paragraph about a time you lost something really important to you. Use a symbol to help the reader understand your attitude toward the loss.

Hyperbole, Symbol, and Irony

Read and think:

[Mrs. Bennett to her husband:] "You take delight in vexing me. You have no compassion for my poor nerves."

[Mr. Bennett to his wife:] "You mistake me, my dear. I have a high respect for your nerves. They are my old friends. I have heard you mention them with consideration these last twenty years at least."

Jane Austen, Pride and Prejudice

Talk about it:

1. Mr. Bennett's reply to his wife is ironic. Is it verbal irony or situational irony? Explain your answer.

2. What is Mr. Bennett's attitude toward his wife? How would it change the reader's understanding of his attitude if he said:

   That is right! I have no compassion for your "poor nerves." I am tired of hearing you talk about your nerves!

Now you try it:

Write a reply to the following accusation:

You never listen to me when I talk to you!

Use verbal irony to express your reply (and your attitude). Model your reply on Austen's use of irony.

Hyperbole, Symbol, and Irony

Read and think:

Two vast and trunkless legs of stone
Stand in the desert...Near them, on the sand,
Half sunk, a shattered visage* lies....
And on the pedestal** these words appear:
"My name is Ozymandias, king of kings:
Look on my works, ye Mighty, and despair!"
Nothing beside remains.

Percy Bysshe Shelley, "Ozymandias"

*face
**the base of the broken statue

Talk about it:

1. This is situational irony. The king had certain expectations. Were these expectations realized? Explain the contrast between what was expected and what actually happened.

2. Look at the sixth line. What does the word "despair" mean? Look the word up to be sure you have an accurate definition. What do you think the king meant by telling other mighty people to "despair"? What do you think the poem means by "despair"? In other words, what does the narrator of the poem want the reader to understand about the meaning of "despair" in this poem?

Now you try it:

Rewrite the poem into a prose paragraph. Your paragraph should *not* contain irony. Instead, it should be just a description of the statue. In other words, there will be no difference between expectations and reality. What effect does your description have on a reader without the irony?

Figurative Language 2: Hyperbole, Symbol, and Irony

Hyperbole, Symbol, and Irony

Read and think:

"Oh, my poor Mathilde! How you are changed!"

"Yes, I have had a pretty hard life, since I last saw you, and great poverty—and that because of you!"

"Of me! How so?"

"Do you remember that diamond necklace you lent me to wear at the ministerial ball?"

"Yes. Well?"

"Well, I lost it."

"What do you mean? You brought it back."

"I brought you back another exactly like it. And it has taken us ten years to pay for it. You can understand that it was not easy for us, for us who had nothing. At last it is ended, and I am very glad."

Madame Forestier had stopped.

"You say that you bought a necklace of diamonds to replace mine?"

"Yes. You never noticed it, then! They were very similar."

And she smiled with a joy that was at once proud and ingenuous.

Madame Forestier, deeply moved, took her hands.

"Oh, my poor Mathilde! Why, my necklace was paste*! It was worth at most only five hundred francs!"

*fake; a cheap copy of diamonds

Guy de Maupassant, "The Diamond Necklace," *Original Short Stories of Maupassant, Volume 4*

Talk about it:

1. This quotation is from a famous story about a young woman who gets invited to a ball. She and her husband have very little money and they sacrifice just to buy her a gown. Then she borrows a beautiful necklace from a rich friend, wears it to the ball, and is much admired and sought-after. The ending of the story, quoted here, is a perfect example of situational irony. Explain the source of surprise: the difference between expectations and reality.

2. Why do you think Maupassant uses irony instead of straightforward description to provide insight into Mathilde's character?

Now you try it:

Think of or make up another story that contains situational irony. Tell your story to a classmate, and identify the difference between expectations and reality, what's intended and what actually turns out to be true.

Write Your Own Figurative Language Lessons on Hyperbole, Symbol, and Irony

Now that you have studied the figurative language lessons on hyperbole, symbol, and irony, it is time for some additional practice. One way to practice is to write your own voice lessons. These pages include quotations you can use to write your own "Talk about it" questions. **Remember that you are not writing comprehension questions.** Instead, you are writing questions that help others understand the power of language: how the author uses hyperbole, symbol, and irony to express voice and to create a world for the reader. To help you write your questions, I have included a hint—a suggestion for focusing your questions. Please do not let the hint limit your questions. Instead, allow your creativity and understanding of the writer's craft lead you to many different places.

You can also write "Now you try it" exercises for each quotation. Remember to use the quote as a model and to design an activity that puts the craft of the quotation into practice.

When you have written questions and exercises, exchange them with other students in your class and try answering each other's questions and exercises. Or you can exchange questions and exercises with members of another class. Discuss the quotations, plan and discuss the questions, practice, and share the craft. This is the way writers learn.

1. Lady Macbeth: ...look like th' innocent flower,
But be the serpent under 't.

William Shakespeare, *Macbeth*, Act I, scene 6

Hint: Focus on the metaphoric and symbolic meaning of the serpent.

2. Paul Bunyan loved dogs as well as the next man but never would have one around that could not earn its keep. Paul's dogs had to work, hunt or catch rats. It took a good dog to kill the rats and mice in Paul's camps for the rodents picked up scraps of the buffalo milk pancakes and grew to be as big as two year old bears.

W. B. Laughead, *The Marvelous Exploits of Paul Bunyan*

Hint: Think about the hyperbole and what it adds to the reader's understanding.

3. But the evil has come with the good, and much fine gold has been corroded. With riches has come inexcusable waste. We have squandered a great part of what we might have used, and have not stopped to conserve the exceeding bounty of nature....

Woodrow Wilson, First Inaugural Address, March 4, 1913

Hint: Look at what the use of gold as a symbol adds to the passage.

4. Mercutio: Ask for me to-morrow, and you shall find me a grave man.

William Shakespeare, *Romeo and Juliet*, Act III, scene 1

Hint: Mercutio says this in the play after he has been seriously hurt in a fight. Look up the word "grave" and think about what a "grave man" is. That would be the literal meaning of the word. Now think about the ironic meaning of the word "grave," what Mercutio really means. Remember, with verbal irony, the speaker says one thing and means another.

Imagery

Introduction

Imagery is the use of words to recreate a sensory experience. People often think imagery refers to creating a visual picture for the reader, but imagery includes any experience with the five senses. In other words, imagery captures in words what we see, what we hear, what we touch, what we smell, and what we taste. Visual imagery is most common, but expert writers experiment with all of the sense experiences in their writing. Imagery is another way to make writing alive and interesting.

It is difficult to separate imagery from diction and detail. In fact, imagery depends on precise word choice and specific detail. The difference lies only in focus: using words and details to capture a sensory experience. Effective imagery is built on effective diction and detail.

Imagery can be figurative or not. If you describe a family dinner as "a combination of boisterous conversation, badly burnt chicken, and the fragrance of freshly baked bread," you would be using imagery but not figurative language. It describes the dinner exactly as it is, and there is no other meaning. If, however, you describe a family dinner as "a *quilt* of boisterous conversation, badly burnt chicken, and the fragrance of freshly baked bread," you would be using imagery that is figurative. A family dinner is not literally a quilt. It is *like* a quilt, combining different sounds, smells, and tastes. It is a metaphor, and the metaphor is developed through imagery.

Imagery, like the other elements of voice, is a tool the writer can use to create a specific experience or feeling. The more specific the imagery is, the more powerful it is as a tool for the writer.

Getting Started with Imagery

Before you begin the imagery exercises, practice creating some specific images. Your images can be figurative or not. Use the chart and topics below.

Topic	Type of imagery	Image
your favorite song	sound	
a sunset	sight	
your favorite kind of pizza	taste	
a bowl of ice	touch	
a fish market	smell	

Imagery

Read and think:

A snug small room; a round table by a cheerful fire; an arm-chair high-backed and old-fashioned, wherein sat the neatest imaginable little elderly lady, in widow's cap, black silk gown, and snowy muslin apron; exactly like what I had fancied Mrs. Fairfax, only less stately and milder looking. She was occupied in knitting; a large cat sat demurely at her feet....

Charlotte Brontë, *Jane Eyre*

Talk about it:

1. Imagery is the reproduction of sensory experiences through language. Which of the five senses (sight, sound, taste, touch, smell) is most important here? Underline the particular words that create this sense experience for the reader?

2. The narrator describes Mrs. Fairfax as "less stately and milder looking" than she imagined. Describe how you think the narrator pictured Mrs. Fairfax before her actual visit.

Now you try it:

Use visual imagery to describe a relative or adult friend of the family. Capture your character's looks, clothes, and surroundings using vivid images. With Brontë's passage as a model, try to set up a contrast between what you expected the character to look like and what the character really looks like.

Imagery

Read and think:

When darkness came on, sky and sea roared and split with the thunder, and blazed with the lightning, that showed the disabled masts fluttering here and there with the rags which the first fury of the tempest had left for its after sport.

Herman Melville, Moby-Dick; or, The Whale

Talk about it:

1. Underline the images. What kind of imagery is used in these lines? What feeling is created by these images?

2. Contrast the feeling created by Melville's sentences with these:

   It got dark and there was a terrible storm. The sails were torn up by the wind.

Now you try it:

Write two sentences describing a scene of calm beauty after a storm has passed. Use both visual and auditory imagery as Melville does in his sentences.

Imagery

Read and think:

Well, after a long time I heard the clock away off in the town go boom—boom—boom—twelve licks; and all still again—stiller than ever. Pretty soon I heard a twig snap down in the dark amongst the trees—something was a-stirring. I sat still and listened.

Mark Twain, The Adventures of Huckleberry Finn

Talk about it:

1. What kind of imagery is used in this passage? How do these images affect the reader?

2. Twain uses imagery to set up a contrast between noise and quiet. List these images in the chart below.

"Quiet" images	"Noise" images

How does the use of both "quiet" and "noise" images shape your understanding of the scene?

Now you try it:

Write a paragraph describing the sounds you hear in your classroom right now. Use imagery that captures both the quiet of the room and the noise of the room. Use Twain's paragraph as a model.

Imagery

Read and think:

It was in the spring of 1890 that I learned to speak. The impulse to utter audible sounds had always been strong within me. I used to make noises, keeping one hand on my throat while the other hand felt the movements of my lips. I was pleased with anything that made a noise and liked to feel the cat purr and the dog bark. I also liked to keep my hand on a singer's throat, or on a piano when it was being played. Before I lost my sight and hearing, I was fast learning to talk, but after my illness it was found that I had ceased to speak because I could not hear. I used to sit in my mother's lap all day long and keep my hands on her face because it amused me to feel the motions of her lips; and I moved my lips, too, although I had forgotten what talking was.

Helen Keller, The Story of My Life

Talk about it:

1. Helen Keller contracted an illness when she was 19 months old that left her blind and deaf. She eventually had a brilliant teacher who taught her to read, write, and speak—experiences that are described in her autobiography. What kind of imagery is most prominent in this paragraph? Support your answer by underlining the images in the paragraph. Are these images figurative or literal? What effect does that have on the reader?

2. What does the imagery in this passage reveal about the character's attitude toward speaking?

Now you try it:

Write a few sentences describing touching something cold and slimy. Use images that appeal to the sense of touch. Do *not* use any figurative language.

Imagery

Read and think:

Some tornadoes look shapeless, like a cloud of dust. Others are very wide. They look like an upside-down bell. Some look like an elephant's trunk. Others are very thin, like a snake. Most tornadoes change shape at some point.

Chris Oxlade, Storm Warning; Tornadoes

Talk about it:

1. Sometimes it's hard to tell the difference between figurative language (like metaphors and similes) and imagery. That's because a lot of figurative language contains imagery. For example, we could describe someone's hair as limp and stringy, like overcooked spaghetti. This is a visual image—it makes you "see" the hair. But it is also figurative (hair is compared to overcooked spaghetti). This paragraph uses figurative language (similes) to give the reader a clear visual image of the different shapes of tornadoes. List the similes used in the passage, and explain the effect the imagery (created by these similes) has on your understanding of tornadoes.

2. Read the passage again and cross out the similes and the visual images they capture. How does the impact of the passage change without the similes?

Now you try it:

Describe two different kinds of cars. First describe the cars using imagery that is figurative. After that, describe the cars with imagery that is literal. Which description do you think is stronger?

Imagery

Read and think:

Going up to the fireplace, he pushed the big kettle aside and reached for a smaller one that was suspended on a chain. Then sitting down on a three-legged stool, he kindled a bright fire. When the kettle was boiling, the old man put a large piece of cheese on a long iron fork, and held it over the fire, turning it to and fro, till it was golden-brown on all sides.

Johanna Spyri, Heidi

Talk about it:

1. Underline the important images in the passage. What kind of imagery do you think is most vivid in this passage? What stands out to you as you read?

2. What feelings do the images in this passage evoke? Would you like to be there?

Now you try it:

Write a paragraph that uses imagery to help the reader understand what something tastes like. Your images can be figurative or not.

Imagery

Read and think:

I crossed the staircase landing, and entered the room she indicated. From that room, too, the daylight was completely excluded, and it had an airless smell that was oppressive. A fire had been lately kindled in the damp old-fashioned grate, and it was more disposed to go out than to burn up, and the reluctant smoke which hung in the room seemed colder than the clearer air,—like our own marsh mist. Certain wintry branches of candles on the high chimney-piece faintly lighted the chamber; or it would be more expressive to say, faintly troubled its darkness.

Charles Dickens, *Great Expectations*

Talk about it:

1. What kind of imagery is used in this passage? Fill in the chart below with images that show which of the five senses Dickens uses to bring the reader into the experience of this passage.

Sight	Sound	Touch	Taste	Smell

2. Consider the last sentence. Which part of the candle description is literal and which is figurative? What kind of figurative language is used here?

Now you try it:

Think of a feast you have enjoyed with family or friends. Using imagery that appeals to sight, smell, and taste, describe the feast to a partner. Your partner should write down several effective images from your description. Switch with your partner and repeat the activity. Share the images with the class.

Imagery

Read and think:

The wild gander leads his flock through the cool night,
Ya-honk he says, and sounds it down to me like an invitation,
The pert* may suppose it meaningless, but I listening close,
Find its purpose and place up there toward the wintry sky.

*flippant

Walt Whitman, "Song of Myself," Leaves of Grass

Talk about it:

1. What kind of imagery is used in these lines? Is the imagery literal or figurative?

2. What is the speaker's attitude toward the gander's cry? How does the imagery in this passage help you understand the speaker's attitude?

Now you try it:

Write four lines of poetry that focus on a sound. It could be a positive sound like the sound of a waterfall or a negative sound like the cry of a friend in danger. Try to create a central sound (like the "ya-honk" in Whitman's poem). Then build your images to reveal your attitude toward the sound.

Imagery

Read and think:

One way to feed water directly to plant roots is drip irrigation. A system of pipes is laid along the ground, close to the plants or just below the surface of the soil. Holes in the pipe allow small amounts of water out into the soil. The water is taken up by plant roots before it evaporates or drains away. This system reduces the quantity of water used for irrigation and reduces water wastage.

Richard Spilsbury, *Managing Water*

Talk about it:

1. Nonfiction uses imagery too. Imagery helps the reader thoroughly understand the information. Read the passage again and sketch an agricultural field with drip irrigation. You are able to do this because of the visual imagery in the passage.

2. Would it be possible to explain drip irrigation without the visual images? Be prepared to defend your answer.

Now you try it:

Think about something you know very well but not everyone understands. Explain what you know using clear, precise visual images. Write at least five sentences. Spilsbury's paragraph can serve as a model.

Imagery

Read and think:

When I reached Richmond, I was completely out of money. I had not a single acquaintance in the place, and, being unused to city ways, I did not know where to go. I applied at several places for lodging, but they all wanted money, and that was what I did not have. Knowing nothing else better to do, I walked the streets. In doing this I passed by many food-stands where fried chicken and half-moon apple pies were piled high and made to present a most tempting appearance. At that time it seemed to me that I would have promised all that I expected to possess in the future to have gotten hold of one of those chicken legs or one of those pies. But I could not get either of these, nor anything else to eat.

Booker T. Washington, Up from Slavery: An Autobiography

Talk about it:

1. Underline all of the images you can find. What kind of imagery is used in this passage?

2. How does the imagery help you understand what the narrator is experiencing?

Now you try it:

Finish the following passage using Washington's paragraph as a model.

I passed by a display of electronic equipment where _____
_____.

Write Your Own Imagery Lessons

Now that you have studied the Imagery lessons, it is time for some additional practice. One way to practice is to write your own voice lessons. These pages include quotations you can use to write your own "Talk about it" questions. **Remember that you are not writing comprehension questions.** Instead, you are writing questions that help others understand the power of language: how the author uses imagery to express voice and to create a world for the reader. To help you write your questions, I have included a hint—a suggestion for focusing your questions. Please do not let the hint limit your questions. Instead, allow your creativity and understanding of the writer's craft lead you to many different places.

You can also write "Now you try it" exercises for each quotation. Remember to use the quote as a model and to design an activity that puts the craft of the quotation into practice.

When you have written questions and exercises, exchange them with other students in your class and try answering each other's questions and exercises. Or you can exchange questions and exercises with members of another class. Discuss the quotations, plan and discuss the questions, practice, and share the craft. This is the way writers learn.

1. Coming from the better part of the fair, I noticed a man who looked like a gentleman farmer, with a young boy by his side; he had a broad back and round shoulders, a kind, ruddy face, and he wore a broad-brimmed hat.

Anna Sewell, *Black Beauty*

Hint: Think about the type of imagery used here and how it helps the reader understand the passage.

2. When it rains here—and it's very apt to rain here every day—it comes down just as if it was a torrent of water. The other night I hung up my hammock in my tent and in the middle of the night there was a terrific storm, and my tent and hammock came down with a run. The water was running over the ground in a sheet, and the mud was knee-deep; so I was a drenched and muddy object when I got to a neighboring tent, where I was given a blanket, in which I rolled up and went to sleep.

There is a funny little lizard that comes into my tent and is quite tame now; he jumps about like a little frog and puffs his throat out. There are ground-doves no bigger than big sparrows, and cuckoos almost as large as crows.

Theodore Roosevelt, *Letters to His Children*

Hint: Focus on how the imagery brings the passage to life.

3. To-day's long march, which, however, has had more road suitable for galloping, has been over wild, weird, desolate, God-forsaken country, interesting from its desolation and its great wastes, forming part of the Kavir or Great Salt Desert of Persia, absolutely solitary, with scarcely a hamlet—miles of the great highway of Persia without a living creature, no house, no bush, nothing. Later, there were some vultures feasting on a dead camel, and a mule-load of two bodies down in the mud.

Isabella L. Bird, *Journeys in Persia and Kurdistan, Volume I*

Hint: Focus on the power of imagery to bring the reader into the experience.

4. He stood, for a moment, with the blood so tingling through all his veins from terror, that he felt as if he were in a burning fire; then, confused and frightened, he took to his heels; and, not knowing what he did, made off as fast as he could lay his feet to the ground.

Charles Dickens, *Oliver Twist*

Hint: Think about how imagery helps the reader know exactly what the character is feeling.

Syntax

Introduction

Syntax is the way words are arranged in sentences. In other words, syntax is the way a writer uses sentence structure to build ideas. Syntax includes these important elements:

- Sentence parts
- Word order
- Sentence length
- Punctuation

Expert writers understand how our language is put together. They learn about language and experiment with the ways we express thoughts and experiences. It's not some dry study of terms and exercises that do not connect to our lives. Quite the contrary, experimenting with syntax is playing with the foundation of communication.

Let's think for a moment about film directors. They have to learn many things about making good films before turning out a masterpiece. There are considerations about focus, props, lighting, animation, movement, foreground, and background. These things take time to master. If you've ever made a video, you know that it's harder than it looks. It is the same with writing. Writers must know their tools and how to use these tools for the best effect. It takes time and practice.

This is not a grammar course. You can write perfectly constructed and interesting sentences without ever knowing what the *subjunctive mood* is. So when you study syntax, don't get caught up with trying to master the fine points of grammar (unless, of course, you find them interesting, in which case there are many wonderful books on grammar). That said, you do need to understand some basic vocabulary in order to understand syntax.

First, you need to understand basic **sentence vocabulary**: subject, verb, clause, phrase, and fragment. Then, you need to understand how writers use these sentence parts to get the effects they want. Finally, you need to have a basic understanding of some very special punctuation marks (specifically, the semicolon, the colon, and the dash) and an important stylistic device (italics). That's all. With these basic tools, you can improve your understanding of the experts' use of language, and you can improve your own expertise with language.

Subjects and Verbs

Let's start with sentence vocabulary. A sentence, as you know, has a **subject** and **verb** and expresses a complete thought. But it can get a little tricky. You have to have some idea of what a subject and verb are. For our purposes, we will keep it pretty simple.

The **subject** is the part of a sentence that expresses what the sentence is about. It's the topic of the sentence.

The **verb** is the part of a sentence that expresses action or connects the subject with the other words in the sentence.

Let's look at a couple of simple sentences as examples:

The lion ran into the wilderness.

First, ask yourself, "What is the sentence about?" The answer, of course, is the lion. That is the subject.

Then ask yourself, "What does the lion do?" or "What is the sentence saying about the lion?" That gives you the verb. The verb here is "ran." It tells you what the lion does. The rest of the sentence is detail.

The lion is a wild animal.

"Lion" again answers the question, "What is the sentence about?" It is the subject.

The lion doesn't do anything in this sentence, so you have to ask the other question: "What is the sentence saying about the lion?" This sentence says that the lion is a wild animal. The verb ("is") connects the subject to whatever the sentence says about the subject. The verb is the connection part. The rest of the sentence is detail.

Clauses and Phrases

Of course, not all sentences are so simple, and sometimes you have to know a little more vocabulary. In addition to subjects and verbs, you should be familiar with larger parts of sentences: **clauses** and **phrases.** Both clauses and phrases are groups of related words, but they have differences.

A **clause** is a group of related words that has a subject and a verb.

A **phrase** is a group of related words that has no subject or verb.

Let's look again at the first sentence above:

The lion ran into the wilderness.

This is a **clause** because it has a subject and verb and is a group of related words.

This is a **phrase** because it is a group of related words but has no subject or verb.

All complete sentences are one or more clauses put together. That's all you need to know.

Sentence Fragments

The last vocabulary term you need to know is **sentence fragment.** A sentence fragment is a group of words that is punctuated like a sentence but is not really a sentence. There may not be a verb, or the words may not express a complete thought. It looks like a sentence but does not meet all of the criteria for being a sentence. Here is an example, building on the earlier sentence:

The lion is a wild animal. Really wild.

This is a sentence fragment. It looks like a sentence because it starts with a capital letter and ends with a period, but it's not. It has no subject or verb, so it can't be a sentence.

You have probably been told never to use sentence fragments in your writing. That's certainly true in very formal writing, but expert writers know how to use sentence fragments and often do.

At its best, a sentence fragment is used for emphasis, to point out the importance of an idea, as in the example above. The fragment "Really wild" makes the reader stop and think about just how wild the lions are. Sentence fragments are powerful in writing but only if you do not overuse them. Be careful about that. It is OK to write a sentence fragment for emphasis, but don't fill your writing with them. Overuse reduces effectiveness. That's a good general rule for syntax.

Word Order

- Now that you have some basic vocabulary, let's talk about word order. The normal word order in English is to have the subject first, then the verb and other details. The sentences on the previous page are in the normal order of the English sentence. But word order is a little more complicated than that. Look at how changing word order changes the meaning in these sentences: Jim said that he drives *only* a truck. (He drives nothing else.)

- Jim said that *only* he drives a truck. (No one else drives a truck.)

- Jim *only* said that he drives a truck. (He probably doesn't really drive a truck.)

- *Only* Jim said that he drives a truck. (No one else said it.)

Amazing, isn't it? Word order is important in English. We learn about word order the same way we learn to talk: by listening. So we don't grow up saying, "Want I water some." We learn in early childhood that we say, "I want some water." Subjects come first, then verbs, then the details. And description words (like *some*) usually come before the words they describe. No one has to explain these things; we just learn them.

While word order in English is pretty inflexible, there is room to change things around. Expert writers sometimes do this for special effect or for emphasis. Look at these sentences:

Am I ever happy about my report card!

Pizza I want—not soup.

The first sentence reverses the order of the subject and the verb. In other words, the verb ("am") comes before the subject ("I"). The second sentence puts the detail ("pizza"—what I want) in front of the subject and verb ("I want"). Putting the words of these sentences in an unusual order catches the reader's attention and emphasizes the ideas. You will learn more about using unusual word order in the Syntax lessons.

Sentence Length

Sentence length is another important part of syntax study. Sentences come in all shapes and sizes from one word ("Help!") to very long and complicated sentences. Writers vary sentence length to keep their readers interested and to control what their readers pay attention to. Most modern writers put the main ideas in short sentences and use longer sentences to expand and develop their main ideas. As you work on the Syntax lessons, you will come to understand how expert writers use sentence length to help the reader understand the written message.

The goal is, always, for you to become more aware of the writing tools you have at hand and how to use them better.

Punctuation and Stylistic Devices

A word about **punctuation**. (Notice that I used a sentence fragment to start this paragraph. I did this for a reason. Many students think that punctuation is a bunch of silly rules made up by adults to use as torture devices. I want you to think about punctuation differently: Punctuation is power in writing! That's why I started this paragraph with a fragment used to catch your attention and emphasize the importance of punctuation.)

Punctuation and stylistic devices help us understand the written word. In speech, we pause and use expression in our voices and on our faces to help the listener understand us. Writing has to depend on punctuation and written style. Punctuation and style help us fine-tune language and say what we really want to say. In this book, we are going to look at the punctuation used most often in shaping voice (the semicolon, colon, and dash) and one stylistic device, italics.

- The **semicolon** joins two or more clauses (complete sentences) when there is no connecting word ("and," "but," "or") or if one of the clauses contains one or more than one comma. When a semicolon is used, all clauses are equally important, and the reader should pay equal attention to them all.

    Example: *He is my best friend; I have known him most of my life.*

- The **colon** tells the reader that something important will follow. It's very important not to confuse the colon and the semicolon. The semicolon shows equal importance, while the colon throws the emphasis onto what comes after it.

    Example: *He is my best friend: He helps me through hard times and celebrates good times with me.*

- The **dash** marks a sudden change in thought or sets off a summary or explanation. Parentheses can do this too, but the dash is more informal and conversational.

    Example: *John—my best friend—lives right down the street.*

- **Italics** are used to emphasize words or phrases. When we handwrite something, we show italics by underlining.

    Example: Of all the people I've *ever* known, John is my best friend.

As you complete the Syntax lessons that follow, you will see many examples of powerful punctuation and style, and you will get better at using punctuation and style for power yourself.

The best way—indeed the only way—to master syntax is to read, read, read. Read the works of expert writers. You'll find that simply by reading, your writing will improve. As you pay attention to the way great writers use sentence structure and punctuation, experiment with syntax in your own writing. That's the way we learn. It's worth the effort: Syntax is a powerful tool for expressing *your* voice.

Syntax

Read and think:

A house divided against itself cannot stand.

I believe this government cannot endure, permanently half slave and half free.

I do not expect the Union to be dissolved—I do not expect the house to fall—but I do expect it will cease to be divided.

It will become all one thing, or all the other.

Abraham Lincoln, "A House Divided" Speech, June 16, 1858

Talk about it:

1. Examine this excerpt from a very famous pre-Civil War speech by Abraham Lincoln. Rate each sentence as short, medium, or long. How does sentence length affect the impact of the passage?

2. Look at the dashes in sentence three. Why do you think Lincoln sets off the clause ("I do not expect the house to fall") with dashes? What purpose does it serve?

Now you try it:

Write three sentences (one short, one medium, and one long) expressing your opinion about cliques in schools. Use Lincoln's sentences as a model.

- In your short, opening sentence, use a metaphor, like Lincoln's "house divided."
- In your medium sentence, use a strong opening clause, followed by a comma and a descriptive phrase.
- In your long sentence, refer back to your metaphor in a clause set off by dashes.

Syntax

Read and think:

He is eloquent and persuasive, and once his words had even power over my heart;
but trust him not. His soul is ... full of treachery and fiend-like malice.

Mary Wollstonecraft Shelley, Frankenstein

Talk about it:

1. Look at the first sentence in this passage. Why do you think Shelley uses a semicolon after
"heart" instead of starting a new sentence?

2. Look at the clause ("trust him not"). How would we say "trust him not" in modern,
everyday English? How does Shelley's unusual word order affect the reader's understanding
of the character?

Now you try it:

Complete the following sentence frame, using Shelley's sentence as a model.

He (or she) is _____ and _____, and once
　　　　　　　　　(adjective)　　　　　　　 (adjective)

his (her) words had even power _____ him (her) not.
　　　　　　　　　　　　　　　　　　 (prepositional phrase)

but _____ .
　　　　　　 (verb)

Syntax

Read and think:

When I had waited a long time, very patiently, without hearing him lie down, I resolved to open a little—a very, very little crevice in the lantern. So I opened it—you cannot imagine how stealthily, stealthily—until, at length, a single dim ray, like the thread of a spider, shot from out the crevice and full upon the vulture eye.

Edgar Allan Poe, "The Tell-Tale Heart," *The Tell-Tale Heart and Other Writings*

Talk about it:

1. Look carefully at the first sentence. There are several groups of words called **phrases** ("very patiently," "without hearing him lie down," "a very, very little") that interrupt the flow of the sentence. Why do you think Poe wrote the sentence like this?

2. Look at the second sentence. What is the purpose of the dashes? How do these dashes, and the words they set off, involve the reader in the action of the passage?

Now you try it:

Write a sentence about doing your chores. Try to imitate the way Poe uses phrases to slow down the way you read the sentence. Use at least one dash.

When I _____

_____

Syntax

Read and think:

She raised her veil as she spoke, and we could see that she was indeed in a pitiable state of agitation, her face all drawn and grey, with restless frightened eyes, like those of some hunted animal. Her features and figure were those of a woman of thirty, but her hair was shot with premature grey, and her expression was weary and haggard. Sherlock Holmes ran her over with one of his quick, all-comprehensive glances.

Sir Arthur Conan Doyle, "The Adventure of the Speckled Band," *The Adventures of Sherlock Holmes*

Talk about it:

1. Examine the first sentence in this passage. Notice that the woman's state of agitation is described with a series of adjective phrases. This is called layering. How does layering help the reader clearly "see" the scene?

2. After the two long, descriptive sentences about the woman, what effect does the use of a short sentence about Sherlock Holmes have on the reader? How does the short sentence help us understand Holmes' character?

Now you try it:

Rewrite the first sentence without the layering, breaking each idea into a separate sentence. How does this rewrite change the impact of the passage?

Syntax

Read and think:

Splendid as can be the blessings of such a peace, high will be its cost: in toil patiently sustained, in help honorably given, in sacrifice calmly borne.

We are called to meet the price of this peace.

Dwight D. Eisenhower, Second Inaugural Address, January 21, 1957

Talk about it:

1. What is the purpose of the colon in the first sentence?

2. Consider the word order of the first part of the first sentence ("Splendid as can be the blessings of such a peace, high will be its cost"). This is not the usual way words are put together in English. What is the usual way? What effect does this unusual syntax have on the reader?

Now you try it:

Write a sentence that uses a colon to connect important ideas. The words that follow the colon should explain and emphasize the words that come before the colon. Use Eisenhower's sentence as a model. Start your sentence this way:

Rewarding as can be acceptance to college, hard will be the years that follow:

_____

_____

Syntax

Read and think:

A nation, like a person, has a body—a body that must be fed and clothed and housed, invigorated and rested, in a manner that measures up to the objectives of our time.

A nation, like a person, has a mind—a mind that must be kept informed and alert, that must know itself, that understands the hopes and the needs of its neighbors—all the other nations that live within the narrowing circle of the world.

And a nation, like a person, has something deeper, something more permanent, something larger than the sum of all its parts. It is that something which matters most to its future—which calls forth the most sacred guarding of its present.

Franklin D. Roosevelt, Third Inaugural Address, January 20, 1941

Talk about it:

1. Read the passage several times. (It's not easy!) What is the purpose of the dashes in this passage?

2. Roosevelt starts each paragraph with similar sentence structure ("A nation, like a person, has..."). What effect does this have on the reader?

Now you try it:

Write three short paragraphs that define a friend. Start each paragraph with a sentence modeled after Roosevelt's (A friend, like a ———, has a ——————.)

Use dashes to extend or explain your thinking.

Syntax

Read and think:

Bears have an amazing sense of smell—perhaps the most sensitive of all animals. They use it to detect threats, mates, and meals. A polar bear can smell a seal that is more than half of a mile away and hidden beneath more than three feet of snow!

Robert Snedden, *Adaptation and Survival*

Talk about it:

1. What is the purpose of the dash in sentence one? What is the purpose of the exclamation point in sentence three?

2. These sentences are very straightforward: very clear, with no unusual word order. Why do you think Snedden chose to write like that?

Now you try it:

Write two clear, straightforward sentences that describe something good about your school. Be very precise and use standard English word order. Use Snedden's sentences as your model.

Syntax

Read and think:

Like sunshine after storm were the peaceful weeks which followed.

Louisa May Alcott, Little Women

Talk about it:

1. What is the subject of the sentence (underline it)? What is the main verb (circle it)? Is this the usual word order of subjects and verbs in English?

2. How does the unusual word order reinforce the meaning of the sentence?

Now you try it:

Reorganize the sentence below. Start with the simile and reverse the standard order of the subject and verb.

Spring break came like a time of calm winds after a hurricane.

Syntax

Read and think:

Little seals can no more swim than little children, but they are unhappy till they learn. The first time that Kotick went down to the sea a wave carried him out beyond his depth, and his big head sank and his little hind flippers flew up exactly as his mother had told him in the song, and if the next wave had not thrown him back again he would have drowned.

Rudyard Kipling, *The Jungle Book*

Talk about it:

1. Look at the two sentences. The first sentence is much shorter than the second. Why do you think Kipling started with a short sentence?

2. How does the form of the second sentence reinforce its meaning?

Now you try it:

Write two sentences describing a fire drill. Your first sentence should be short, introducing the main idea. Your second sentence should be longer, and it should imitate the meaning with its form.

Syntax

Read and think:

The Great Society rests on abundance and liberty for all. It demands an end to poverty and racial injustice, to which we are totally committed in our time. But that is just the beginning.

The Great Society is a place where every child can find knowledge to enrich his mind and to enlarge his talents. It is a place where leisure is a welcome chance to build and reflect, not a feared cause of boredom and restlessness. It is a place where the city of man serves not only the needs of the body and the demands of commerce but the desire for beauty and the hunger for community....

But most of all, the Great Society is not a safe harbor, a resting place, a final objective, a finished work. It is a challenge constantly renewed, beckoning us toward a destiny where the meaning of our lives matches the marvelous products of our labor.

Lyndon Baines Johnson, Remarks at the University of Michigan, May 22, 1964

Talk about it:

1. In this passage Lyndon Baines Johnson defines the Great Society (how he envisions the United States). How does the syntax of the passage clarify his definition? Look especially at sentence length and repeated sentence patterns.

2. How would the impact of this passage change if Johnson had simply said the following?

   The Great Society will end poverty, support education, encourage people to appreciate beauty and get along, and make work meaningful.

Now you try it:

In three paragraphs, define an abstract idea (like love, school pride, popularity, freedom, or friendship). Using Johnson's passage as a model, define what your abstraction is and is not. Repeat the sentence pattern "it is..." at least three times.

Write Your Own Syntax Lessons

Now that you have studied the Syntax lessons, it is time for some additional practice. One way to practice is to write your own voice lessons. These pages include quotations you can use to write your own "Talk about it" questions. **Remember that you are not writing comprehension questions.** Instead, you are writing questions that help others understand the power of language: how the author uses syntax to express voice and to create a world for the reader. To help you write your questions, I have included a hint—a suggestion for focusing your questions. Please do not let the hint limit your questions. Instead, allow your creativity and understanding of the writer's craft lead you to many different places.

You can also write "Now you try it" exercises for each quotation. Remember to use the quote as a model and to design an activity that puts the craft of the quotation into practice.

When you have written questions and exercises, exchange them with other students in your class and try answering each other's questions and exercises. Or you can exchange questions and exercises with members of another class. Discuss the quotations, plan and discuss the questions, practice, and share the craft. This is the way writers learn.

1. Miss Cowley left the delights (and drudgeries*) of her home life early in the war and came up to London, where she entered an officers' hospital. First month: Washed up six hundred and forty-eight plates every day. Second month: Promoted to drying aforesaid plates. Third month: Promoted to peeling potatoes. Fourth month: Promoted to cutting bread and butter.

Agatha Christie, *The Secret Adversary*

*hard work; chores

Hint: Focus on the effective use of sentence fragments.

2. Happiness lies not in the mere possession of money; it lies in the joy of achievement, in the thrill of creative effort.

Franklin D. Roosevelt, First Inaugural Address, March 4, 1933

Hint: Focus on the use of the semicolon.

3. The Amazon River is the world's widest and deepest river. It contains 60 times more water than the River Nile. It runs for 7,100 km (4,410 miles), from its source in Peru 6,500 m (21,330 ft.) up in the Andes Mountains, down to sea level at the Atlantic coast. The Amazon drainage basin covers the entire central and eastern region of South America.

Richard Spilsbury, *Managing Water*

Hint: Look at sentence length.

4. The man [Captain Hook] was not wholly evil; he loved flowers (I have been told) and sweet music (he was himself no mean performer on the harpsichord); and, let it be frankly admitted, the idyllic nature of the scene stirred him profoundly. Mastered by his better self he would have returned reluctantly up the tree, but for one thing.

What stayed him was Peter's impertinent appearance as he slept. The open mouth, the drooping arm, the arched knee: they were such a personification of cockiness as, taken together, will never again, one may hope, be presented to eyes so sensitive to their offensiveness. They steeled Hook's heart.

J. M. Barrie, *Peter Pan*

Hint: Focus on the creative use of punctuation, parenthetical clauses, and sentence length.

Tone

Introduction

We examine tone last because understanding tone requires an understanding of all the elements writers use to create it: diction, detail, figurative language, imagery, and syntax. Tone can be a little difficult to identify at first, but the elements of voice you have already studied will help you, and you will get better with practice.

So, what is tone? **Tone** is the expression of the author's **attitude** toward his or her audience and subject matter. It can also be the expression of the speaker or narrator's attitude toward his or her listener or subject matter. And sometimes it's a little of both. It is the **feeling** that grows out of the material, the feeling that the writer creates for the reader. There are as many different tones as there are feelings: serious, lighthearted, playful, sarcastic, accepting, and so forth. The trick is to be able to identify tone in reading and create tone in writing.

It's easy to understand tone in spoken language. If your mother says, "Don't use that tone of voice with me!," you know exactly what she means. You have expressed a disrespectful feeling through *what you said* but especially *how* you said it. And you understand her tone all too well: She is angry with you. We understand tone in speech by listening not only to words but to the way words are said and by seeing the facial expressions of those who say them.

Here's another example. Take the single word "right" and consider the many different ways you can say it to suggest an attitude. See if you can express the different attitudes that underlie the word "right" listed below. Work with a partner.

Right?	Is this right?
Right!	You're absolutely right.
Right!	This won't happen.
Right.	I heard you, but I don't believe you.
Right!	Turn right, not left!

It's harder to understand and create tone in writing since you can't depend on vocal and facial expressions. But it can be done. Just as we understand tone in speech from *what* is said and *how* it's said, the same is true in writing. It just takes more practice to see it. We create tone in writing through all of the elements of voice:

1. Diction
2. Detail
3. Figurative language
4. Imagery
5. Syntax

In these tone exercises, you will learn to understand the *what* and *how* of tone and to create tone in your own writing.

As you work with the tone exercises, you will need three types of practice:

1. Practice figuring out the tone of a passage,

2. Practice explaining how you know the tone of a passage, and

3. Practice writing passages in which you create a certain tone.

All of these skills will get easier with time and attention to the elements of voice.

To discuss tone, you need to develop a **tone vocabulary.** You need practice in figuring out *what* the tone is and *how* that tone is created. On the following page is a beginning list of tone words. As you discuss the tone of passages here and in your other reading, keep adding to the list.

Understanding tone is both challenging and fascinating. When you understand tone in reading, you can connect to the writer's thoughts and experiences and how the writer works to craft an effect. That's what close reading is all about! When you understand and practice creating tone, you can say exactly what you want to say in writing. You can build the precise experience you want your reader to have. And that's what writing's all about! Good luck to all of you.

Tone Words

abusive	disparaging	peaceful
accepting	disrespectful	pessimistic
acerbic	doubtful	playful
admiring	dry	pragmatic
affectionate	enthusiastic	questioning
angry	eulogistic	reproachful
anxious	exhilarated	respectful
apprehensive	facetious	rueful
approving	fearful	sad
ardent	flippant	sarcastic
awestruck	forceful	sardonic
biting	frightening	satirical
bitter	grim	sentimental
brisk	harsh	serious
bristling	haughty	severe
brusque	humorous	sharp
calm	hypercritical	silly
cavalier	indifferent	somber
censorious	indignant	straightforward
cold	ironic	strident
complimentary	irreverent	subdued
confident	joyful	sympathetic
confused	laudatory	thoughtful
contemptuous	lighthearted	threatening
conversational	loving	trenchant
critical	melancholy	uncertain
cutting	mistrustful	understated
cynical	mocking	whimsical
defamatory	mysterious	withering
denunciatory	neutral	wry
detached	nostalgic	
disdainful	objective	

Additional Tone Words

Tone

Read and think:

...Yes, one of the brightest gems in the New England weather is the dazzling uncertainty of it.... You fix up for the drought; you leave your umbrella in the house and sally out, and two to one you get drowned. You make up your mind that the earthquake is due; you stand from under, and take hold of something to steady yourself, and the first thing you know you get struck by lightning. These are great disappointments; but they can't be helped. The lightning there is peculiar; it is so convincing, that when it strikes a thing it doesn't leave enough of that thing behind for you to tell whether—Well, you'd think it was something valuable, and a Congressman had been there. And the thunder. When the thunder begins to merely tune up and scrape and saw, and key up the instruments for the performance, strangers say, "Why, what awful thunder you have here!" But when the baton is raised and the real concert begins, you'll find that stranger down in the cellar with his head in the ash-barrel....I could speak volumes about the inhuman perversity of the New England weather, but I will give but a single specimen. I like to hear rain on a tin roof. So I covered part of my roof with tin, with an eye to that luxury. Well, sir, do you think it ever rains on that tin? No, sir; skips it every time.

Mark Twain, "The Weather," Address at the New England Society's Seventy First Annual Dinner, New York City, *Speeches of Mark Twain*

Talk about it:

1. This passage is from the first part of a speech by Mark Twain about New England weather. What is the tone of the passage? Brainstorm tone words that fit this passage and add new words to your "Tone Words" list.

2. How do you know the tone of this passage? Use the following chart to fill in the evidence for what you identify as the tone of this passage. Discuss your chart.

Diction What specific words help create the tone?	Detail What details add to the tone?	Figurative Language What figures of speech help create the tone?	Imagery What images help create the tone?	Syntax How does the sentence structure help create the tone?

Now you try it:

Write a paragraph about the weather in your part of the country. In your paragraph, create a tone similar to Twain's. Pay careful attention to the elements of voice that create the tone.

Tone

Read and think:

Mind, in this speech I have been trying merely to do honor to the New England weather—no language could do it justice. But, after all, there is [sic] at least one or two things about that weather (or, if you please, effects produced by it) which we residents would not like to part with. If we hadn't our bewitching autumn foliage, we should still have to credit the weather with one feature which compensates for all its bullying vagaries—the ice-storm: when a leafless tree is clothed with ice from the bottom to the top—ice that is as bright and clear as crystal; when every bough and twig is strung with ice-beads, frozen dew-drops, and the whole tree sparkles cold and white, like the Shah of Persia's diamond plume. Then the wind waves the branches and the sun comes out and turns all those myriads of beads and drops to prisms that glow and burn and flash with all manner of colored fires, which change and change again with inconceivable rapidity from blue to red, from red to green, and green to gold—the tree becomes a spraying fountain, a very explosion of dazzling jewels; and it stands there the acme, the climax, the supremest possibility in art or nature, of bewildering, intoxicating, intolerable magnificence. One cannot make the words too strong.

Mark Twain, "The Weather," Address at the New England Society's Seventy First Annual Dinner, New York City, *Speeches of Mark Twain*

Talk about it:

1. This passage is the second part of a speech by Mark Twain about New England weather. What is the tone of this part of the speech? What tone words describe this passage? If you think of new words, add them to the "Tone Words" list.

2. How does Twain create a new tone in this part of his speech? What transition marks the change? Underline the diction, detail, imagery, and figurative language that help create the tone. Discuss how the syntax in this passage helps create the tone.

Now you try it:

Look at the description of weather you wrote in the previous exercise. Now shift the tone as you describe something particularly beautiful you can experience in the weather in your part of the country. Use Twain's passage as a model and pay particular attention to diction, detail, figurative language, and imagery.

Tone

Read and think:

MIRANDA: O, wonder!
How many goodly creatures are there here!
How beauteous mankind is! O brave* new world
That has such people in't!

William Shakespeare, *The Tempest*

*wonderful, impressive

Talk about it:

1. What is the tone of this passage? How do you know?

2. How would the tone of the passage change if we simply changed the punctuation like this?

   MIRANDA: O, wonder.
   How many goodly creatures are there here?
   How beauteous mankind is. O brave new world
   That has such people in't.

Now you try it:

Write a similar passage in praise of your favorite singer or athlete. Your tone should be admiring. Use your own, natural language. Focus on the use of punctuation to create the tone.

Tone

Read and think:

My mother, I suppose, attracted the attention of a purchaser who was afterward my owner and hers. Her addition to the slave family attracted about as much attention as the purchase of a new horse or cow. Of my father I know even less than of my mother. I do not even know his name. I have heard reports to the effect that he was a white man who lived on one of the near-by plantations. Whoever he was, I never heard of his taking the least interest in me or providing in any way for my rearing. But I do not find especial fault with him. He was simply another unfortunate victim of the institution which the Nation unhappily had engrafted upon it at that time.

Booker T. Washington, *Up From Slavery: An Autobiography*

Talk about it:

1. What is the tone of the passage? Think carefully about this; it may not be obvious on the first reading.

2. How does Washington use syntax to create the tone of this passage?

Now you try it:

Write a sentence about your favorite team losing a soccer game. This sentence should be matter of fact, with a neutral, nonjudgmental tone. Now write a sentence about your team losing that has an angry, judgmental tone. Pay attention to how you create the tone.

Tone

Read and think:

OBSOLETE, adj. No longer used by the timid. Said chiefly of words. A word which some lexicographer* has marked obsolete is ever thereafter an object of dread and loathing to the fool writer, but if it is a good word and has no exact modern equivalent equally good, it is good enough for the good writer.

Ambrose Bierce, *The Devil's Dictionary*

*someone who writes dictionaries

Talk about it:

1. Look up the definition of "obsolete" in a regular dictionary. Now read Bierce's definition again. How are the two definitions different?

2. What is Bierce's attitude toward someone defining words as obsolete? How do you know? Explain how Bierce's diction helps you identify his attitude.

Now you try it:

Write a short definition of *homework*. In your definition, choose words that clearly reveal your attitude toward homework. Use Bierce's definition as a model.

Tone

Read and think:

I have always thought that all men should be free; but if any should be slaves, it should be first those who desire it for themselves, and secondly those who desire it for others. Whenever I hear any one arguing for slavery, I feel a strong impulse to see it tried on him personally.

Abraham Lincoln, "From an Address to an Indiana Regiment. March 17, 1865," *Speeches and Letters of Abraham Lincoln, 1832–1865*

Talk about it:

1. What is Lincoln's attitude toward slavery? How does he convey this attitude?

2. How would the tone and power of the passage change if it were written like this?

   I believe in freedom. If anyone argues for slavery, he should become a slave himself.

Now you try it:

Write a sentence about bullying modeled after Lincoln's first sentence above. Try to use the same tone as Lincoln does.

Tone

Read and think:

'You should learn not to make personal remarks,' Alice said with some severity; 'it's very rude.'

The Hatter opened his eyes very wide on hearing this; but all he SAID was, 'Why is a raven like a writing-desk?'

'Come, we shall have some fun now!' thought Alice. 'I'm glad they've begun asking riddles.— I believe I can guess that,' she added aloud.

'Do you mean that you think you can find out the answer to it?' said the March Hare.

'Exactly so,' said Alice.

'Then you should say what you mean,' the March Hare went on.

'I do,' Alice hastily replied; 'at least—at least I mean what I say—that's the same thing, you know.'

'Not the same thing a bit!' said the Hatter. 'You might just as well say that "I see what I eat" is the same thing as "I eat what I see"!'

'You might just as well say,' added the March Hare, 'that "I like what I get" is the same thing as "I get what I like"!'

'You might just as well say,' added the Dormouse, who seemed to be talking in his sleep, 'that "I breathe when I sleep" is the same thing as "I sleep when I breathe"!'

Lewis Carroll, *Alice's Adventures in Wonderland*

Talk about it:

1. In the highlighted section above, there is an argument about whether or not word order matters. What attitude about the importance of exact word order underlies this argument? How do you know?

2. What is the tone of the passage? How does Carroll create the tone?

Now you try it:

Consider this statement: *Thinking about doing something illegal is the same thing as doing something illegal.* Now argue against the statement using at least two examples. Start each example with the statement, "You might as well say…." Keep your tone fairly neutral.

Tone

Read and think:

In an effort to increase their share of trade, supermarkets regularly undercut one another's prices. This is good for shoppers, but it makes things difficult for farmers, both in developing countries and in the developed world. Since the 1980s, many farmers have been forced out of business by the ultra-low prices supermarkets offer for their food.

Supermarkets also set very high standards for the food they buy. Fruits and vegetables that are not of an exact size and shape, or free of all blemishes, are often rejected. This leads to enormous waste.

Jen Green, The Impact of Environmentalism: Food and Farming

Talk about it:

1. What is the author's attitude toward supermarkets? How do you know?

2. What is the tone of this passage? What helped you to determine the tone?

Now you try it:

Write a paragraph about fast-food restaurants. Create your own tone with diction, detail, and syntax.

Tone

Read and think:

And so, my fellow Americans: ask not what your country can do for you—ask what you can do for your country.

My fellow citizens of the world: ask not what America will do for you, but what together we can do for the freedom of man.

John F. Kennedy, Inaugural Address, January 20, 1961

Talk about it:

1. What is the tone of the passage? Add any new tone words to the class list.

2. Examine and discuss how the syntax in this passage shapes the tone. Pay particular attention to the following:

Syntax	How it shapes the tone
Starting the first sentence with "And so."	
The colon in the first sentence	
The reversal of the usual word order ("ask not" instead of "do not ask")	
The dash in the first sentence	
The colon in the second sentence	
Sentence length	

Now you try it:

Write a sentence that gives some solid advice to a friend. Try to create a similar tone to Kennedy's, and model the syntax of your sentence on his sentences.

Tone

Read and think:

"You see—you see," she panted, "if no one knows but ourselves—if there was a door, hidden somewhere under the ivy—if there was—and we could find it; and if we could slip through it together and shut it behind us, and no one knew anyone was inside and we called it our garden and pretended that—that we were missel thrushes* and it was our nest, and if we played there almost every day and dug and planted seeds and made it all come alive—"

*birds common in Europe

Frances Hodgson Burnett, *The Secret Garden*

Talk about it:

1. What is the tone of the passage? Add any new tone words to your "Tone Words" list.

2. How do diction, detail, imagery, figurative language, and syntax create the tone?

Now you try it:

Write a few sentences about a place you hope to visit. Create a tone of anticipation and exhilaration. Use at least two "if" clauses to create the feeling of breathlessness and eagerness like Burnett does.

Write Your Own Tone Lessons

Now that you have studied the Tone lessons, it is time for some additional practice. One way to practice is to write your own voice lessons. These pages include quotations you can use to write your own "Talk about it" questions. **Remember that you are not writing comprehension questions.** Instead, you are writing questions that help others understand the power of language: how the author uses tone to express attitude and to create a world for the reader. To help you write your questions, I have included a hint—a suggestion for focusing your questions. Please do not let the hint limit your questions. Instead, allow your creativity and understanding of the writer's craft lead you to many different places.

You can also write "Now you try it" exercises for each quotation. Remember to use the quote as a model and to design an activity that puts the craft of the quotation into practice.

When you have written questions and exercises, exchange them with other students in your class and try answering each other's questions and exercises. Or you can exchange questions and exercises with members of another class. Discuss the quotations, plan and discuss the questions, practice, and share the craft. This is the way writers learn.

1. Stranger, if you passing meet me and desire to speak to me, why should you not speak to me?
And why should I not speak to you?

Walt Whitman, "To You," Leaves of Grass

Hint: Focus on how syntax (especially word order) creates the tone.

2. Our landscape is shaped by **weathering** and **erosion**. Weathering happens when natural forces, such as water, temperature, and wind, break down rocks on the Earth's surface. Erosion is when the rock pieces are washed or blown away. Soft rocks like clay and sandstone are more easily weathered and eroded than harder rocks, such as granite.

Richard Spilsbury, Managing Water

Hint: Think about how informational text uses tone and how diction, detail, and sentence length shape the tone. Remember that informational text aims for clarity and the tone is often neutral.

3. The gentleness of the honey-bee, when kindly treated, and managed by those who properly understand its instincts, has in this treatise been frequently spoken of, and is truly astonishing. They will, especially in swarming time, or whenever they are gorged with honey, allow any amount of handling which does not hurt them, without the slightest show of anger. For the gratification of others, I have frequently taken them up, by handfuls, suffered them to run over my face, and even smoothed down their glossy backs as they rested on my person!

Rev. L. L. Langstroth, Langstroth on the Hive and the Honey Bee, A Bee Keeper's Manual

Hint: Focus on how the use of detail creates the tone.

4. Romeo: But, soft! What light through yonder window breaks?
It is the east, and Juliet is the sun.
Arise, fair sun, and kill the envious moon,
Who is already sick and pale with grief,
That thou her maid art far more fair than she....

William Shakespeare, *Romeo and Juliet*, Act II, scene 2

Hint: Look at how Shakespeare uses figurative language to create the tone.

Additional Activities for Teaching Voice

Diction Contest
Have students collect words that catch their attention from outside reading—newspapers, novels, magazines. Give a monthly prize for the best word.

Delve into Diction
Have students nominate and vote for three words per week to study in detail.

Intensity Ladder
Take a concept word (sadness, happiness, fear) and brainstorm related words with different degrees of meaning. Have students make an intensity ladder showing the words associated with the concepts, from the mildest to the most intense.

Visualization
Have students close their eyes as you take them on an imaginary walk. Ask them to focus on all of the details they "see" on their walk. Later, have them list the details and write a description of their walk.

Detail through Pictures
Show students a series of pictures. Then have them examine the details using the following chart:

Who?	What?	When?	Where?	Why?	How?

Figurative Language Contest

Give a prize to the student who collects the most examples of figurative language in a week. Students can collect figurative language from newspapers, magazines, or their independent reading. They should write down the quote, identify the type of figurative language, and identify where the quote came from.

Irony and Comics

Have students look for irony in comics from the newspaper. For extra credit, students can paste the comic on a piece of paper and explain the irony.

Metaphor of the Day

Pick an abstract word of the day (things that are important to students: friends, video games, family, social media, pets, tests, sports, homework), and have students write metaphors that say something fresh and original about the word.

Imagery Picture

Have students think of an event that was so important to them that it changed their lives. Then have them draw a picture containing something they saw, tasted, heard, smelled, and touched while that event was going on.

Syntax in the Headlines

Have students cut out headlines from the newspaper, cutting each word separately, and put the cut-up headlines in zipper bags. Students can then exchange bags and put the words from the headlines in the correct order. It's not as easy as it sounds! Discuss the syntactic clues that make one way to put the words in order better than another and how changing the word order changes the meaning of the headline.

Teacher's Tone

Write or say sentences that capture something you feel strongly about, and ask students to identify the tone of the sentences.

Tone Word of the Week

Put the tone words from the chart in a hat and have a student pick one for a tone of the week. Discuss the tone and how students can create it in writing. Then have students write daily sentences using the tone of the week.

Beach Ball Analysis

Randomly write the following words on a beach ball:

- Diction
- Detail
- Imagery
- Syntax
- Figurative Language
- Tone

Select a passage—a paragraph or a few lines of poetry—and have students read it carefully several times. Toss the ball to a student. When the student catches the ball, tell him or her to look at the word that is closest to his or her right thumb. The student must then analyze the use of that element of voice in the selected passage.

Capturing the Spoken Voice

Have students listen to a partner talk about a great video game or movie for one minute and write what his or her partner said, trying to capture the partner's voice. Students should then read what they wrote aloud and discuss this question: Does it still sound like your partner? Students should look for the specific diction, detail, imagery, figurative language, and syntax that make the writing sound like spoken English.

Writing with Voice

Use this exercise to help students understand how to write with voice. Stress the importance of voice in writing and help students understand that they can control the effect they have on their readers. It takes experimentation and practice, but it is well worth the effort.

Read the **skeleton description** of a situation below:

I ate lunch at the mall. The food was terrible. The table was dirty. The company was fantastic.

The purpose of this exercise is to write about the situation in a clear, developed voice of your own. To do this, complete the following steps:

1. Think about your own voice—how do you express your personality when you talk? Discuss this with a partner.

2. Think about how you can express your **talking personality** *in writing* as you fully describe the skeleton description above. Discuss this with a partner.

3. Describe your **talking voice** *in writing*.

4. Talk to a partner *in that voice* about the situation.

5. Write about the situation using your **talking voice.**

6. Share.

After you have drafted your piece, answer these questions and discuss your answers with a partner:

1. Does your written piece sound like your **talking voice?**

2. How did you recreate your **talking voice** in writing? (What was the process?)

3. What writing tools did you use to create your voice? (What were your techniques?)

Revise and rewrite your piece, paying careful attention to the tools of voice.

Other student-friendly **skeleton descriptions:**

- *I had lots of homework. My best friend called and wanted me to go out. I had to think about it.*

- *My mother's friend came over for dinner. I do not like my mother's friend.*

- *It was after curfew. The lights were still on in my house.*

- *My best friend is mad at me. It wasn't my fault. I wish this hadn't happened.*

- *I went to the movie with my friend. The movie was great. My friend was a pain.*

Discussion Suggestions

Please note: These are my suggested answers to the "Talk about it" questions. They are suggestions only and by no means exhaust the possible responses to the questions. My intent is to spark discussion and encourage thinking. I fully acknowledge and recognize you, the classroom teacher, as the expert, and I honor your ideas and insights. ND

Diction

Carl Sandburg, "How the Five Rusty Rats Helped Find a New Village," *Rootabaga Stories* (p. 12)

1. "The wind changed black" is a vivid and fresh way to describe the growing intensity of the storm. A black wind implies danger and fury with no ray of light to guide the characters. By using a color word to describe something that we cannot actually see, Sandburg focuses the reader's attention on the feeling of the wind, its ominous character, rather than merely the physical nature of the wind. Creating the atmosphere associated with the wind helps the reader fully visualize the scene as it looks and feels.

2. The intensity is gone. We do not know how hard the wind blew, and we do not get a feeling of the storm's fury and danger. The new sentence does not let the reader fully participate in the experience of the storm.

Frances Hodgson Burnett, *The Secret Garden* (p. 14)

1. These strong verbs denote fast action, movement almost free from gravity. In addition, the verbs have a strong connotation of excitement and an urgency to arrive at a destination (supported also by the verbs "unchained," "unbolted," and "unlocked," transitive verbs that do not even seem to have time for a direct object).

2. Here it has a positive connotation. While the sun pouring down on one can be a most uncomfortable experience, here it is not. The connotation is established by the surrounding description. She is excited to get outside; the grass has suddenly turned green, a sure sign of a welcome spring; the air is sweet and warm; and the birds are singing. The sun is lovely after a harsh winter. Note that the writer does not have to explain this—the reader understands the connotation from the diction.

Jules Verne, *Around the World in Eighty Days* (p. 15)

1. A tree, like an animal, is described as a skeleton because it is dead. The life—the leaves and outer bark—has dropped from the tree. But the word "skeleton" also has a connotation of desolation and emptiness. It imparts a feeling of danger and impending doom to the scene (the characters, too, might become skeletons). The freshness of the diction (applied to a tree) surprises the reader and helps him or her understand the intensity of the scene. The denotation of the word "white" is that the tree is covered with snow. The whiteness also has a connotation: it reinforces the tree's barrenness and ghost-like appearance, creating a mood of mysterious danger. The diction creates both a physical scene and a feeling for the reader, imparting a full experience of the action.

2. The wolves are hungry. They are "gaunt," or extremely thin, and "famished," or extremely hungry. An animal that is starving is highly motivated to catch anything it can eat. By describing the wolves as gaunt and famished, Verne helps the reader to actively participate in the scene. These are not idle wolves, curious about the sled. They are actively chasing the sled, spurred on by starvation.

Jack London, *The Call of the Wild* (p. 16)

1. The setting here is in the extreme north, where the aurora borealis glows green and soft red. The word "flaming" thus refers to the colors of fire and the word "coldly" refers to the temperature. It makes sense here. But it does more than make sense. The unusual juxtaposition of words helps the reader understand the severity of the weather. Cold and hot seem to merge; flames do not indicate warmth.

2. The "defiance of life" connotes great strength and refusal to submit to adversity. On the other hand, the "pleading of life" connotes submission, relinquishing control, and begging for another force to provide survival. The argument that the huskies' song is "pleading of life" is supported by the diction: The song is "pitched in a minor key" (generally sorrowful); the song contains "long-drawn wailings and half-sobs." This choice of words indicates a sadness, desperation, and loss of control, a begging for mercy in life's dangers.

Rudyard Kipling, "How the Leopard Got His Spots," *Just So Stories* (p. 17)

1. "Scuttle" means to scurry or move with short, hurried movements. "Trudge" means to walk heavily, to plod. The pictures these verbs create are totally different. "Scuttle" creates a picture of light-footed animals moving with energy and speed. It also creates a feeling of nervous movement. "Trudge," on the other hand, creates a feeling of heaviness, of slow, burdened walking. The feeling associated with "trudge" is not one of nervousness; rather, it is one of slow discouragement.

2. The hyphenated adjectives help create the mood of the scene. The shadows are emphasized since they help create the blotchiness of the giraffe, the zebra's stripes, and darkness of Eland. The first hyphenated adjective ("patchy-blatchy") emphasizes the shadows through rhyme as well as the use of a nonsense word. This directs the reader's attention to the nature of the shadows—their intermittent shade and their eventual importance. The second hyphenated adjective ("slippery-slidy") uses alliteration to draw attention to the shadows. Here the repeated *sl*- sound evokes the sounds and mystery of the forest and the elusive nature of the forest's protection.

Oscar Wilde, "The Happy Prince," *The Happy Prince and Other Tales* (p. 18)

1. The young man is poor. The evidence for this is in the diction. First, he is in a "garret," an attic room, usually associated with a struggling artist of some kind. His "violets" are in a "tumbler," not a vase, and they are "withered," a certain sign of distress. Also, Wilde was obviously aware of the literary associations of violets. Although violets are prized for their fragrance, they are spring flowers and usually die by summer. Thus, they are often associated in literature with death (look at Ophelia's madness scene in *Hamlet*). The fact that the violets here are withered reinforces that association. You may want to explain this association to the class during the discussion. Although death and poverty are not, of course, always related, this passage certainly gives a feeling of the fading hope of poverty.

2. "Crisp" creates a picture of hair that is brittle and stands up around his face. However, a less common definition of "crisp" means having small curls or waves. It could mean that. Give students lots of leeway in their sketches. The purpose of this question is to help students think deeply about the pictures words create, keeping in mind the mood already established in the first two sentences.

Dwight D. Eisenhower, Second Inaugural Address, January 21, 1957 (p. 19)

1. The basic meaning of the sentences does not change. However, the impact of the sentences changes drastically. Through the use of strong verbs, Eisenhower captures the teeming abundance of America's industry and productivity. The rivers, rails, skies, harbors, and highways are "crowded" with commerce, giving the feeling of great energy and plenty. The air "rings" with the song of industry, giving a picture of beauty rather than clamor and pollution. The linking verbs ("are," "is") in the changed sentences lack the power to evoke connotation as well as denotation.

2. The reader (or listener to this speech) expects to hear "America the Beautiful," the title of a song most Americans know well. By substituting "bountiful" for the expected "beautiful" and surprising the reader (listener), Eisenhower clearly conveys the attitude he has already suggested: that America is a land of industry, business, productivity, and plenty. Beauty is secondary.

O. Henry, "The Lonesome Road," *41 Stories by O. Henry* (p. 20)

1. The words "pistoled" and "spurred" simply mean wearing a pistol and spurs. However, using the nouns as adjectives creates a more vivid picture. Caperton is *adorned* with the pistol and spurs. The unusual usage focuses the reader's attention on the pistol and spurs, which become central to the character's tough image and strength.

2. The word "indefeasible," used to describe Caperton, establishes the character as unconquerable. This character is as permanent and unchanging as a well-written law. Using "indefeasible" in this way reinforces the strength of the character and helps the reader understand the character's nature.

Chris Oxlade, Storm Warning: Tornadoes (p. 21)

1. An anvil is used for working metal. Anvils are made of very hard steel, hard enough to receive great force. They are flat on top for working metal but taper down to a narrower base.

   Students' sketches should be of clouds that have flat tops and are tapered beneath.

2. The new sentence uses only denotative meaning. The tops are flat. However, by calling them "anvil tops," Oxlade evokes both denotative and connotative meaning. Anvils do have flat tops. But anvils are also very strong and capable of receiving great force. This enriches the impact of the description. Tornadoes are also very strong and capable of receiving great force (e.g., lightning or updrafts). You may have to explain this part to the class. The enriched meaning helps the reader understand the nature of tornado thunderclouds.

Charles Dickens, David Copperfield (p. 22)

1. Students' charts should look something like this:

Words that tell you the room is cold	Words that tell you the room is dark
hoar frost	fog
rimy	ghostly
clammy	dim
breath...wreathing and smoking	sputtering candle
raw cold	foggy
they blow upon their fingers	
tap their feet	

2. A "sputtering" candle is burning poorly—making spitting and popping sounds—not burning smoothly. In other words, there is a serious draft in the room and the candle is in danger of going out. The sputtering candle reinforces the cold, dark, drafty feeling of the schoolroom. The only warmth and light is a sputtering candle, which is not much. The feeling of the room, then, is one of poverty and despair and implies that the lives of those who inhabit this room are bleak indeed, without adequate warmth and light.

Detail

Walt Whitman, "The Runner," *Leaves of Grass* (p. 27)

1. Students should underline such details as these:

    > On a flat road runs the well-train'd runner,
    > He is lean and sinewy with muscular legs,
    > He is thinly clothed, he leans forward as he runs,
    > With lightly closed fists and arms partially rais'd.

    All of these details help the reader see the runner himself. They are effective in focusing the reader's attention on the runner by excluding details about the race, audience, weather, or any other possible focus. The details function like a camera lens, placing the runner in sharp focus and relegating all possible competing details to a blur.

2. Students can choose from among the rich details in the poem. Although some details seem fairly neutral ("thinly clothed," "leans forward," "lightly closed fists," "arms partially rais'd"), students may have fun with changing these details to change the meaning. Other details ("well-train'd," "lean and sinewy," "muscular") are clearly positive, and students can also change these details to change the meaning. Students may want to completely rewrite the poem, changing all of the details to negative ones.

Richard Spilsbury, *Managing Water* (p. 28)

1. The main idea of this paragraph is stated in the first sentence: "The rapidly expanding world population is a major pressure on water availability." There are many details that support and strengthen the main idea: World population is rapidly growing, especially in countries such as Pakistan and Nigeria; rates of usage are increasing; improved sanitation requires water (washing machines, showers, baths, flushing toilets).

2. The changed paragraph contains no evidence or support for its general statements. There is no detail. By leaving out the detail, the paragraph loses its credibility. In nonfiction, as in fiction, believability is dependent on the use of adequate, concrete detail. The detail moves the text from abstraction to specificity, lending authority and plausibility to the description.

O. Henry, "The Ransom of Red Chief" (p. 29)

1. The main idea or focus of the paragraph is stated simply in the first sentence: "I was awakened by a series of awful screams from Bill." Or students could word it more indirectly, e.g., "The narrator says that he was awakened by Bill's awful screams." The details turn this simple statement into a colorful, vivid description of the very nature of the screams. The narrator explains what the screams are not, as well as what they are. In this way, he shapes the reader's understanding of the passage.

2. The details humanize the screamer, Bill. He is strong, which makes the screaming seem real. Then the narrator calls Bill fat, not the usual way one would describe a warrior or (in this case) a kidnapper out for ransom. The detail lends some humor to the description with an ironic contrast between what the reader would expect and what is happening.

Franklin D. Roosevelt, First Inaugural Address, March 4, 1933 (p. 30)

1. There are all kinds of fear. Roosevelt makes it clear exactly what he means by fear through detail. He talks about "nameless" fear—fear that cannot even be identified. He talks about "unreasoning" fear—fear that has no basis in rational thought. He talks about "unjustified" terror—terror that is not based in a sensible response to concrete danger. Further, he talks about fear that paralyzes one's power to go forward. Through detail, the reader is brought into the same understanding of fear that Roosevelt has.

2. Without the detail, the statement lacks passion, strength, and clarity. The reader has no full understanding of what fear is in this context, and the reader is not brought into the exact experience and understanding of the speaker.

Frederick Douglass, *Narrative of the Life of Frederick Douglass, An American Slave* (p. 31)

1. Students' contributions will vary. As students offer details they remember most, be certain they provide evidence and reasons for why they find particular details memorable.

2. The details that help the reader understand Douglass' happiness are underlined below:

I found employment, the third day after my arrival, in stowing a sloop with a load of oil. It was new, dirty, and hard work for me; but I went at it with a glad heart and a willing hand. I was now my own master. It was a happy moment, the rapture of which can be understood only by those who have been slaves. It was the first work, the reward of which was to be entirely my own. There was no Master Hugh standing ready, the moment I earned the money, to rob me of it. I worked that day with a pleasure I had never before experienced. I was at work for myself and newly-married wife. It was to me the starting-point of a new existence.

The details clearly express his joy, but underlying each detail is the contrast of his present work with the pain and horror of slavery. These details allow the reader to participate in Douglass' happiness at being free, but the details also help the reader to understand the context: what he had to suffer in order to find this happiness.

Robert Louis Stevenson, *Treasure Island* (p. 32)

1. The original is, of course, more alive and engrossing, bringing the reader into the scene. Instead of just missing a leg, his left leg is "cut off close by the hip." He "carried" a crutch, which implies he did not always need it. And he hops about on the crutch "like a bird," with "wonderful dexterity." The details make the passage real and give the reader a chance to visualize the character in a concrete and precise way.

2. Students' sketches will vary. What is most important is to discuss why they chose certain details: What made the details memorable? It will be interesting to see if most students choose the same details or if there is variety in the sketches. The important lesson, of course, is that the details allow students to clearly picture Long John and to sketch him.

J. M. Barrie, *Peter Pan* (p. 33)

1. A number of words would do: "magical," "enchanted," "charmed," "mysterious," "picturesque," "lovely." These words are supported by all of the details of the passage: You have to shut your eyes and be lucky to see the lagoon; the colors change from pale to fiery as you squeeze your eyes tighter; the moment is "heavenly" when you see the lagoon; you might have a chance to see the surf and hear the mermaids.

2. The details of the passage take the reader deeper and deeper into the scene. It's like sharing a secret with the narrator. The narrator gives the reader a way to see the lagoon (shutting your eyes and squeezing them tighter), then only allows you to see it for one moment. Then the narrator offers the tantalizing possibility of seeing the surf and hearing the mermaids. The details intensify the scene, personalize the relationship between reader and narrator, and make the reader feel the same admiration and awe as the speaker.

Isabella L. Bird, *A Lady's Life in the Rocky Mountains* (p. 34)

1. Students' charts should look something like this:

the air	the snow	the sky	her physical condition
"fierce heat" "highly rarefied"	"so pure and dazzling that I was obliged to keep my eyes shut as much as possible to avoid snow blindness"	"the light too dazzling" "the sun too fierce" "a different and terribly fierce color" "the sun, he was white and unwinking"	"I felt as if I should drop off the horse" "the fierce heat caused soul and sense, brain and eye, to reel" "nausea" "exhaustion" "pains from head to foot" "must lie down"

2. Bird has a clear focus (the discomfort of her day) supported by specific detail about the discomfort. Shifting focus and including too much detail can detract from the impact of the paragraph. Also, too much unrelated detail can overwhelm the reader and turn a description into a catalogue, without focus or purpose. By selecting specific detail to support her purpose and avoiding other details, Bird creates a clear picture, supports her purpose, and controls the reader's focus.

Helen Keller, *The Story of My Life* (p. 35)

1. The experiences described in this paragraph obviously take place before Keller learns to read, write, and speak. First, she describes the days "before [her] teacher came." Then she uses detail to capture her discomfort with the world: "fit of temper," the need to "find comfort," the need "to hide [her] hot face in the cool leaves and grass."

2. The paragraph would lose its power and distance the reader from the action. The rewrite *explains* Keller's experiences instead of allowing the reader to *see* the scene through vivid detail. Explaining or telling rather than creating an experience for the reader is a common error of inexperienced writers, and it is important for students to see the difference. Keller *creates* the experience through detail; the rewrite *tells* about it. Students will easily see which one is more alive and engaging.

Sir Arthur Conan Doyle, *The Sign of the Four* (p. 36)

1. Sherlock Holmes is a strong character, careful, observant, and highly intelligent. Details that support this include: he "led the way"; he "carefully examined marks which appeared to me to be mere shapeless smudges"; "he walked slowly...shooting keen glances to right and left." He is also not one to hurry or panic. ("He walked slowly from step to step...")

2. The rewrite lacks interest and focus. It is general, abstract, and bland. It loses the detail that brings the character (Holmes) to life and helps the reader to fully understand the character's nature. The detail in the original paragraph focuses the reader's attention on how the specific characteristics of Holmes take shape in a story. Detail gives life to abstraction and helps the reader participate in exactly the understanding that the author intends.

Figurative Language 1: Metaphor, Simile, and Personification

Isabella Bird, *A Lady's Life in the Rocky Mountains* (p. 42)

1. Several examples of figurative language in the passage are identified in the chart below. We know the language is figurative because the words cannot be taken literally. As with all figures of speech, one thing is literally said and another is meant.

Figure of speech	Metaphor or simile?	How you know
"sailing orders"	Metaphor	She is riding a horse, not sailing, so we know it must be figurative rather than literal. The land she is traversing is the prairie: lots of open space, grass undulating to the wind, trails going everywhere. It is reminiscent of the sea. The use of a nautical metaphor helps the reader understand the nature and feeling of the prairie (wild, open, unpredictable). It is a metaphor because the comparison is implied rather than stated.
"steer south"	Metaphor	Again, the language is figurative, not literal. We don't use the word "steer" to describe horseback riding. This metaphor carries out the previous metaphor, extending the comparison of the prairie with the sea. It is a metaphor because the comparison is implied, not directly stated.
"like embarking on the ocean without a compass"	Simile	In keeping with the two previous metaphors, this simile compares riding through the prairie to sailing on the ocean (without a compass!). The simile captures the open spaces, the feeling of vastness, and the difficulty of finding the way. It is a simile because the comparison is directly stated.
"rolling brown waves"	Metaphor	Here Bird compares the grass to ocean waves. In fact, if you have ever crossed the prairie, the grass does move much like an ocean wave. This metaphor (implied) continues the comparison with the sea and helps the reader visualize the prairie.

2. The figurative language adds depth and clarity to the passage, making it far more alive and vivid than it would have been without the figurative language. By using metaphors and similes, Bird can tap the associations we have with the sea and use these associations to help the reader participate in her experience of traveling across the prairie. Metaphors and similes, then, allow a writer to say more with fewer words and to create an experience more succinctly and convincingly.

Alfred Noyes, "The Highwayman" (p. 43)

1. The metaphor in this stanza is "His eyes were hollows of madness." The literal term is "eyes," and the figurative term is "hollows of madness." Roughly translated, the metaphor means that Tim has eyes that are deep-set and have a crazed look to them. But the metaphor goes far beyond a translation. His eyes don't just take on the quality of madness. They *are* madness, deep and frightening. By calling his eyes "hollows," Noyes evokes the picture of a deep well or cave, an emptiness and darkness that haunts the reader. The metaphor says far more than a simple description could.

2. Here are the similes:

Line #	Simile	Figurative term	Literal term
3	"his hair [was] like mouldy hay"	mouldy hay	hair
6	"dumb as a dog"	dog	dumb (his inability to speak)

Although most dogs are certainly not stupid, which could make the reader question this simile, the simile uses the word "dumb" in another sense, meaning without human speech or being intentionally silent. So through this simile, we can see Tim as almost inhuman and a sneaky, manipulative beast. Further, by comparing Tim to a dog, Noyes also calls up many of a dog's potentially negative qualities: dirty, snarling, vicious, ready for a fight. A simile, like a metaphor, provides lots of detail and insight in few words.

Abraham Lincoln, The Gettysburg Address (p. 44)

1. The implied metaphor is contained in these words: "our fathers brought forth upon this continent a new nation, conceived in liberty." It is a complex metaphor. The fundamental comparison is between the creation of a new nation and the conception and birth of a child.

2. The literal term is the new nation. The figurative term (which is suggested rather than stated) is the conception and birth of a child. The metaphor is developed in several ways: Our "fathers," the founders of the country, [bring] "forth," engender, the nation as a father produces a child.

H. G. Wells, *The Time Machine* (p. 45)

1. "Like one who was trying to keep hold of an idea that eluded him" is not a simile. In fact, it is not figurative at all. The Time Traveller really *does* speak like someone "who was trying to keep hold of an idea that eluded him." It is descriptive, not figurative. Two essentially unlike things are not being compared. The existence of a comparison or the words "as" or "like" does not automatically mean there is a simile. If I say, "She looks like her mother," I am speaking literally since she *does* look like her mother. There is nothing nonliteral about the comparison.

2. Students will come up with lots of creative ways to act out the sentences. It would be helpful to have them write some metaphors or similes to make the scene more vivid and engaging. They can use their similes from the "Now you try it" exercise.

William Shakespeare, *As You Like It*, Act II, scene 7 (p. 46)

1. The figurative term that goes with "all the world" (all of life, the literal term) is the "stage"; the figurative term that goes with "all the men and women" (the literal term) is "players." In other words, Shakespeare is saying that life is like a play being performed on a stage and all people are simply actors in the play.

2. Lines three and four extend and develop the metaphor. The players have their "entrances" (birth, new beginnings of all kinds) and "exits" (death, endings of all kinds). Each player plays many parts (as in life). It would be interesting to have students discuss all of the parts they have learned to play so far in their lives (student, child, friend, athlete, etc.). The extended metaphor inspires that kind of discussion, allowing readers to look at abstractions (life and death) in a fresh and thought-provoking way.

Robert Snedden, *DNA and Genetic Engineering* (p. 47)

1. The sentence is a simile. The comparison is directly stated. The words "can be thought of as" indicate an explicit comparison.

2. The literal term is "a cell's DNA" and the figurative term is "an instruction manual." Snedden extends the simile by comparing a gene to the plan for a specific part (a metaphor). This extension is a metaphor since the comparison is implied and an identification is set up (each gene *is* a part's plan).

William Jefferson Clinton, Second Inaugural Address, January 20, 1993 (p. 48)

1. The simile in the passage is [Martin Luther King was] "like a prophet of old." The literal term is "Martin Luther King," and the figurative term is "a prophet of old."

2. The meaning of the passage is enriched by this simile. By comparing King to a prophet of old, Clinton is able to include many ideas in few words: King is wise, clairvoyant, a true leader. Figurative language has the power to bring multiple meanings sharply and succinctly into writing. In addition, figurative language helps the reader visualize the passage, a powerful tool for deep comprehension.

George Bernard Shaw, *Pygmalion*, Act 3 (p. 49)

1. The two things being compared are the way Clara looks at Eliza and a beast eating something fiercely. The literal term is implied: the way Clara looks at Eliza ("with her eyes"). The figurative term is also implied: a beast eating something fiercely ("devouring her"). Clara is looking at every detail of Eliza: her face, her hair, her dress, her shoes, the way she sits and talks.

2. Without the metaphor, the stage directions would be flat and imprecise. The metaphor allows the reader to clearly visualize what the action should look like. We use this kind of language all of the time and never think of it as figurative, but it is. Instead of a long sentence describing Clara looking at Eliza, Shaw uses a metaphor that promotes economy and the power of words.

Kenneth Grahame, *The Wind in the Willows* (p. 50)

1. Students' charts should look like this:

Example of personification	Literal term	Figurative term
"the ruddy brick floor smiled up at the smoky ceiling"	floor	person smiling
"the oaken settles, shiny with long wear, exchanged cheerful glances with each other"	settles	people exchanging cheerful glances
"plates on the dresser grinned at pots on the shelf"	plates	people grinning
"merry firelight flickered and played over everything without distinction"	firelight	a merry, playful person

2. The use of personification helps the reader visualize the scene by attributing familiar human actions (smiling, cheerful glancing, grinning) to inanimate objects. Because of this, the reader can better understand the feeling of the scene (cheery and warm). In addition, personification provides a human connection, helping the reader relate to the scene.

These examples are pretty straightforward except for the last one. Firelight *does* flicker; however, firelight cannot be merry or playful. Firelight is thus personified.

Samuel Taylor Coleridge, "The Rime of the Ancient Mariner" (p. 51)

1. The personification is underlined below:

> And now the <u>Storm-blast came, and he</u>
> <u>Was tyrannous and strong</u>:

The literal term is the "Storm-blast." The figurative term is a "tyrannous and strong" man. Remember that the figurative term in personification is always human or human-like.

2. This line is a little problematic. The literal term is still the "Storm-blast." And there is still a "he" involved as the figurative term. However, the "he" has "o'ertaking wings," not exactly a human trait. I visualize it as a human-like figure—large, powerful, and relentless—with wings. In this case, it would still be personification. But students could also make a good argument for this to be a metaphor, with the figurative term a fierce bird. It might be a good time for some group discussion and lively debate.

Figurative Language 2: Hyperbole, Symbol, and Irony

Lewis Carroll, *Alice's Adventures in Wonderland* (p. 57)

1. Since a hyperbole is a form of figurative language, the purpose is to add meaning and provide understanding through a nonliteral use of language. Alice saying she would "think nothing of tumbling down stairs" and would say nothing even if she "fell off the top of the house" is saying that she has become very, very brave about falling after tumbling down the rabbit hole. But it's a far more vivid way of saying it. Hyperboles are rarely misunderstood or taken literally because they take the nonliteral sense of the words to such an extreme. But they add color and interest to language.

2. The original sentence is, of course, the one that helps the reader understand what Alice is thinking. It helps the reader see just how traumatic the original fall was and how brave she feels for enduring it. By using a hyperbole, we get a glimpse into Alice's character. The rewrite is a bland, general summary.

Oscar Wilde, *The Picture of Dorian Gray* (p. 58)

1. The hyperbole is the whole sentence. It is an exaggeration in the service of truth. Wilde states that there are only two kinds of fascinating people. Of course there are many more than that. Also, no one knows everything and no one knows nothing. Wilde is again using a hyperbole.

2. All hyperboles are grounded in some sort of truth—at least to the narrator or author. Here the truth that underlies the hyperbole is that the narrator finds people who know a lot and people who know very little fascinating. He could have just said that, but the exaggeration is much more thought provoking. What makes such people so interesting? The hyperbole gets the reader's attention and emphasizes ideas.

Robert Burns, "A Red, Red Rose" (p. 59)

1. The hyperbole is underlined below:

    As fair art thou, my bonnie lass,
    So deep in luve am I:
    And I will luve thee still, my dear,
    <u>Till a' the seas gang dry.</u>

    Remember that a hyperbole is figurative, nonliteral. The figurative part is "Till a' the seas gang dry." Of course all of the seas won't go dry. It is exaggeration in the service of truth.

2. The speaker's attitude toward his "bonnie lass" is one of deep, undying love. The hyperbole, although exaggeration, emphasizes this point and helps reveal the truth underlying the exaggeration—that the speaker is in love and believes that his love for her will last for all time.

Mark Twain, *The Adventures of Tom Sawyer* (p. 60)

1. I would call it a hyperbole. Although we can feel that "life is hollow" and "existence but a burden" when faced with a difficult, tedious task, painting a fence does not literally make life hollow and existence a burden. It is exaggeration in the service of truth.

2. The hyperbole in the last sentence is "the far-reaching continent of unwhitewashed fence." The figurative term is the "far-reaching continent." The hyperbole (of course the unpainted part of the fence is not as large as a continent) reveals Tom's attitude far more vividly than a simple description could. To Tom, the part of the fence left to paint seems like an entire continent. The task seems endless.

William Shakespeare, *Henry IV, Part II*, Act III, scene 1 (p. 61)

1. The "something else" is the power and duty of a king. Wearing a crown, or being a king, can overwhelm a man with worries and concerns, making it difficult for him to rest easily.

2. The new line has none of the power and interest of the original. It explains rather than lets the reader explore the idea. The crown is a traditional symbol of royalty, used often in literature (and art) over time. It calls forth all of the associations of royalty: power, duty, wealth, concern for the country, concern for succession, and so on. With a symbol like this, meaning is enriched and intensified. Additionally, in this case, the rewritten sentence totally destroys the meter and beauty of Shakespeare's line.

Francis Scott Key, "The Star-Spangled Banner" (p. 62)

1. The flag in these famous lines from our national anthem symbolizes America: the original colonies and the 50 states. But more than that, the flag has become a symbol of the country itself, its heritage and character. Calling the flag "the star-spangled banner" deepens our understanding of its symbolic value. The stars are shining brightly and the flag is waving—a sign to all that America will prevail.

2. "The rocket's red glare" is not a symbol. Remember that a symbol is itself and something else. There is no "something else" here. This is descriptive language, a detail.

Queen Elizabeth I, Speech to the Troops at Tilbury, 1588 (p. 63)

1. Blood is a complex traditional symbol. Throughout history, in literature and art, blood has come to symbolize life itself—vitality and passion—the physical life force. It has also come to symbolize heritage, as in bloodline. So in this passage, blood is literal (Elizabeth is willing to shed her blood—die—for her troops) but it is something else as well. The "something else" is her vitality, her royalty, her heritage as a queen. She is willing to sacrifice that as well.

2. The use of blood as a symbol helps the reader understand Elizabeth's attitude toward her country and her troops. She is willing to make the ultimate sacrifice for them. The use of blood as a symbol—both as life force and heritage—compresses and intensifies the meaning and allows the reader to understand her total dedication to her troops and her country.

Jane Austen, *Pride and Prejudice* (p. 64)

1. This is verbal irony. Mr. Bennett says one thing and means the opposite. When he calls his wife's nerves (the way she gets upset and complains about everything) his "old friends," he is suggesting familiarity but not fondness or respect. He is clearly tired of her nervousness, but he does tolerate his wife. Her "poor nerves" are his "old friends" only in that her nervous condition has been around for at least 20 years. The reply is not, however, sarcastic. The intent is lighthearted humor rather than hurtful criticism. Mr. Bennett is gently making fun of his wife, but there is an underlying acceptance, perhaps resignation, rather than the disgust implicit in sarcasm.

2. Mr. Bennett's attitude toward his wife is patronizing, lightly critical, but accepting. The new sentence totally changes the expression of attitude. The irony is gone and so is the complexity of the response. Now the attitude implicit in the response is clearly one of criticism and anger. There is no humor or acceptance.

Percy Bysshe Shelley, "Ozymandias" (p. 65)

1. The king's expectations were not realized. (In situational irony, things always turn out in a way other than expected.) The king thought his power and fame (expressed by the large statue and its inscription) would be lasting. However, the statue and, by implication, the king's power and influence lie in the desert in ruins.

2. The king calls himself "king of kings" and commands other mighty people to look at his accomplishments and "despair" (They should despair, give up hope, because they will never have such great and lasting accomplishments.). We understand from lines 1–3 and line 7 that the king's works have turned out differently than expected. This is situational irony. His accomplishments are nothing; a ruined statue in the sand. So "despair" takes on a different meaning in the poem. The "mighty" that come after Ozymandias should despair not because they cannot be as great as Ozymandias; but they should despair because power, pride, and kingdoms ultimately amount to nothing.

Guy de Maupassant, "The Diamond Necklace," *Original Short Stories of Maupassant, Volume 4* (p. 66)

1. If students do not understand the surprise, have them read the passage again. The surprise is that the necklace, which Mathilde and her husband thought was valuable and sacrificed for ten years to pay for, was a fake and worth very little money. They expected that the necklace Mathilde borrowed had real diamonds, and they replaced it with a real diamond necklace, which took ten years to pay off. The reality was that the necklace was a fake and their sacrifice was needless.

2. The use of irony provides sharp insight into Mathilde's character. Had Maupassant simply described her as proud and vain, the character would not have been memorable. Instead, the story reveals her character through irony. She could have told her friend of the loss, and she would not have had to sacrifice for ten years. The situational irony reinforces the needlessness of the sacrifice, the senseless pride of the character, and the unpredictability of life itself.

Imagery

Charlotte Brontë, Jane Eyre (p. 71)

1. Visual imagery (sight) is most important here. Here are the particular words students can underline:

A snug small room; a round table by a cheerful fire; an arm-chair high-backed and old-fashioned, wherein sat the neatest imaginable little elderly lady, in widow's cap, black silk gown, and snowy muslin apron; exactly like what I had fancied Mrs. Fairfax, only less stately and milder looking. She was occupied in knitting; a large cat sat demurely at her feet....

Note that most of the paragraph is composed of images, which make the scene come alive for the reader.

2. Students can come up with a variety of answers. They need to examine what "stately" and "milder looking" mean and what Mrs. Fairfax would look like if she were more stately and less mild.

Herman Melville, Moby-Dick; or, The Whale (p. 72)

1. The imagery here is both visual (sight) and auditory (sound). Students should underline these images:

When darkness came on (visual), sky and sea roared and split with the thunder (auditory), and blazed with the lightning (visual), that showed the disabled masts fluttering here and there with the rags which the first fury of the tempest had left for its after sport (visual).

The imagery creates a feeling of danger and fury. There is darkness, lightning, and thunder, and it is intense. The sea and sky "roar" and "split" with thunder, creating a feeling of total destruction; the sky "blazes" with lightning, capturing a feeling of further destruction through fire. And the masts and sails are already destroyed by the storm, creating a feeling of desperation and desolation.

2. There is little vivid imagery in the rewritten lines. The lines lack power to bring the reader into the scene. Instead, the feeling of these lines is abstract and general. "It got dark" has no sense of foreboding, unlike "darkness came on" (as if it had a will of its own). The storm is only described in general terms (i.e., "there was a terrible storm"). The lines have lost their ability to evoke an experience for the reader.

Mark Twain, *The Adventures of Huckleberry Finn* (p. 73)

1. This passage is dominated by sound (auditory) imagery. The images create the experience for the reader and bring the reader into the scene.

2. Students' charts should look something like this:

"Quiet" images	"Noise" images
"all still again—stiller than ever" "I sat still and listened"	"I heard the clock away off in the town go boom— boom—boom—twelve licks" "I heard a twig snap" "something was a-stirring"

The contrast between the "quiet" and "noise" imagery emphasizes the feelings of tension in the passage. Although noise is slight or far away, the "something a-stirring" is threatening because of the contrasting silence. The imagery helps create the tension of watchfulness and wariness of being alone.

Helen Keller, *The Story of My Life* (p. 74)

1. The most prominent imagery in the paragraph is tactile. This was the primary way that Helen Keller perceived the world around her. Although there is some auditory imagery ("audible sounds"; "I used to make noise"), the dominant and most vivid imagery is tactile. Tactile images are underlined below:

It was in the spring of 1890 that I learned to speak. The impulse to utter audible sounds had always been strong within me. I used to make noises, keeping one hand on my throat while the other hand felt the movements of my lips. I was pleased with anything that made a noise and liked to feel the cat purr and the dog bark. I also liked to keep my hand on a singer's throat, or on a piano when it was being played. Before I lost my sight and hearing, I was fast learning to talk, but after my illness it was found that I had ceased to speak because I could not hear. I used to sit in my mother's lap all day long and keep my hands on her face because it amused me to feel the motions of her lips; and I moved my lips, too, although I had forgotten what talking was.

The images are not figurative. The language is literal and descriptive. The tactile images help the reader understand exactly what Keller experienced. The images also enable the reader to closely approximate the personal knowledge Keller has of perception through touch. Further, the images help the reader understand the importance of our senses in both understanding the world and in writing.

2. The imagery in this passage helps the reader understand Keller's attitude toward speaking, which is one of fascination, admiration, and longing. The reader can feel her touching a cat to experience its purring, touching a singer's throat or a piano, and touching her mother's lips as her mother talks. The imagery makes the passage come alive and allows the reader to understand Keller's deep attraction to speech.

Chris Oxlade, *Storm Warning: Tornadoes* (p. 75)

1. The similes include "like a cloud of dust," "like an upside-down bell," "like an elephant's trunk," and "like a snake." All of these similes help the reader picture the different shapes of tornadoes, making the similes also visual images. By using similes to compare the shapes of clouds to other familiar objects, Oxlade helps the reader clearly visualize the clouds.

2. Without the similes (and the visual imagery), the reader cannot clearly "see" the clouds. They are "shapeless," "wide," or "thin." The description is general and uninteresting. The passage loses its ability to present a clear mental picture for the reader.

Johanna Spyri, *Heidi* (p. 76)

1. Students should underline these images:

> Going up to the fireplace, he pushed the big kettle aside and reached for a smaller one that was suspended on a chain. Then <u>sitting down on a three-legged stool</u>, he kindled a <u>bright fire</u>. When the kettle was boiling, <u>the old man put a large piece of cheese on a long iron fork</u>, and held it over the fire, turning it to and fro, till it was golden-brown on all sides.

Visual imagery is important in the passage, allowing the reader to "see" the old man as he prepares a fire and a simple meal. However, to me, the most vivid and lasting imagery of the passage is that of smell and taste. The reader can almost smell the cheese browning. And although taste is not specifically mentioned in the text, through association of smell and taste, the reader can almost taste the toasted cheese straight from the "long iron fork." Students may have different opinions here. They should focus on the imagery that touches them personally and brings them into the scene.

2. The passage evokes feelings of comfort and warmth. There is nothing threatening or alarming in any of the imagery. The fire is "bright"; the simple meal is inviting. I would certainly like to be there, although some students may find it a bit too rustic.

Charles Dickens, *Great Expectations* (p. 77)

1. The chart should look something like this:

Sight	Sound	Touch	Taste	Smell
"I crossed the staircase landing, and entered the room she indicated"	The only sound is an implied sense of silence	"the reluctant smoke which hung in the room seemed colder than the clearer air,—like our own marsh mist"	none	"it had an airless smell that was oppressive"
"the daylight was completely excluded"				
"A fire had been lately kindled in the damp old-fashioned grate, and it was more disposed to go out than to burn up"				
"wintry branches of candles on the high chimney-piece faintly lighted the chamber"				

2. The literal part of the candle description is "certain...candles on the high chimney-piece faintly lighted the chamber." There are parts of this visual image, however, that are figurative. Calling the candles "wintry branches" is a metaphor, allowing the reader to see the candles as white and frail branches of trees, stripped of life (leaves). The candles are also personified. They "troubled its [chamber's] darkness," giving the reader a feeling that the darkness is so oppressive that the light of the candles is like a person "faintly" disturbing the darkness, insignificant and inadequate.

Walt Whitman, "Song of Myself," *Leaves of Grass* (p. 78)

1. The imagery in these lines is mainly auditory, supported by visual and tactile imagery. The imagery is literal.

2. The speaker's attitude toward the gander's cry is one of awe and respect. An auditory image creates the gander's cry, providing the sound itself rather than a description of it and bringing the reader into the scene. The gander is "wild" and "leads his flock through the cool night." The sound of the gander's cry is an "invitation," and the speaker "finds its purpose and place [in the] wintry sky." The images are serene and reverent, clearly conveying the speaker's attitude.

Richard Spilsbury, *Managing Water* (p. 79)

1. Students' sketches should include the pipes, plants, a suggestion of soil, holes in the pipes, and water. This would be a good time to stress the importance of text-dependent answers to questions. Students cannot draw drip irrigation without careful reading of the visual imagery provided in the text.

2. The visual images are extremely important. But it might be interesting to describe drip irrigation with only tactile images. See if your students can accept this challenge!

Booker T. Washington, *Up from Slavery: An Autobiography* (p. 80)

1. Here are the underlined images in the passage:

> When I reached Richmond, I was completely out of money. I had not a single acquaintance in the place, and, being unused to city ways, I did not know where to go. I applied at several places for lodging, but they all wanted money, and that was what I did not have. Knowing nothing else better to do, I walked the streets. In doing this I passed by many food-stands where fried chicken and half-moon apple pies were piled high and made to present a most tempting appearance. At that time it seemed to me that I would have promised all that I expected to possess in the future to have gotten hold of one of those chicken legs or one of those pies. But I could not get either of these, nor anything else to eat.

The imagery is mostly visual (and not figurative), but the description also evokes the smell of the food by describing the unrequited longing Washington has for the food.

2. The imagery brings the reader into the experience. We can "see" Washington walking the streets, trying to find lodging and food. We can "see" the food piled high and "smell" its aroma, a sharp contrast to Washington's hopelessness, desperation, and poverty.

Abraham Lincoln, "A House Divided" Speech, June 16, 1858 (p. 87)

1. Sentence one is short, sentence two is medium, sentence three is long, and sentence four is short again. In general, writers state main ideas in short sentences and elaboration in longer sentences. By starting with a short sentence, Lincoln makes a clear, dramatic statement of his claim (the metaphor strengthens his claim as well). His second and third sentences are elaboration, developing his claim (and continuing the metaphor). The use of a short sentence again at the end of the passage emphasizes his claim and brings his argument to a close, echoing the first sentence but not repeating or summarizing.

2. Dashes often indicate a sudden change in thought. Here Lincoln breaks up his sentence and goes back to the metaphor to emphasize his point that the union will not be dissolved. The clause that is set off by dashes is closely related to the rest of the sentence but breaks the flow of the sentence with a shift back to the metaphor. Lincoln is talking to "the people" in a speech. The dashes indicate an informal and conversational tone and reinforce his connection with his audience.

Mary Wollstonecraft Shelley, *Frankenstein* (p. 88)

1. A semicolon indicates equal importance to both parts of the sentence. The description before the semicolon is positive ("eloquent," "persuasive," "his words had even power over my heart"). However, this description is balanced by the negative impact of the clause after the semicolon ("but trust him not"). Since the semicolon gives equal weight to both parts of the sentence, both ideas are true: He is persuasive and eloquent, but he is also untrustworthy. The semicolon balances ideas and helps the reader understand the complexity of the character and the narrator's response to the character.

2. We would say, "Do not trust him," in modern, everyday English. The unusual word order catches the reader's attention and emphasizes the word "not," negating the trust with a short, definitive sentence ending. [Students may wonder why "trust him not" is a clause. It contains a subject and verb and expresses a complete thought. The subject of the clause is understood ("you," since the sentence contains the imperative mood); the verb is "trust." "Him" is the direct object of the verb.]

Edgar Allan Poe, "The Tell-Tale Heart," *The Tell-Tale Heart and Other Writings* (p. 89)

1. By interrupting the flow of the sentence with phrases, Poe slows down the movement of the sentence and increases the tension. The reader has to wait for the action to unfold. The words advance as slowly as the action itself.

2. A dash marks a sudden change of thought, a brief summary, or a parenthetical remark that is emphasized. The dashes in this sentence set off a direct address to the reader and slow down the sentence, creating apprehension for the reader. The parenthetical address to the reader increases the tension of the sentence and involves the reader directly in the action by forcing the reader to wait for the slow, secretive actions revealed by the sentence.

Sir Arthur Conan Doyle, "The Adventure of the Speckled Band," *The Adventures of Sherlock Holmes* (p. 90)

1. Layering intensifies the description. Each adjective phrase builds on the one before and gives the reader a vivid picture of the woman's agitation. The description starts with a general statement ("she was indeed in a pitiable state of agitation") but becomes more and more specific as the sentence continues ("her face all drawn and grey," "with restless frightened eyes"). The sentence ends with a simile, comparing her eyes to those of "some hunted animal." By going from the general to more specific to very specific (the simile), Doyle gives a clear picture of the woman, just as the writer wants the reader to perceive her. The syntax controls our experience of the woman and allows us to focus on one detail at a time.

2. The short sentence about Sherlock Holmes focuses the reader's attention on his character. Holmes does not need elaborate description. Just as he views the woman "with one of his quick, all-comprehensive glances," the reader can understand his character quickly and sharply from a short sentence. Syntax reinforces meaning.

Dwight D. Eisenhower, Second Inaugural Address, January 21, 1957 (p. 91)

1. A colon serves to emphasize what follows. It may direct the reader's attention to a brief summary or explanation, or it may direct attention to an amplification of what comes before the colon. Here, the colon amplifies or explains the cost of peace. Specifically, maintaining peace will take work, help, and sacrifice. The emphasis of the sentence is not on the blessings of peace but on the cost, as indicated by the colon.

2. The more usual word order would be: "The blessings of such a peace can be splendid, but its cost will be high." The unusual syntax catches the reader's (or listener's) attention. It also draws attention to the words "splendid" and "high" by placing them first in each clause. It prepares the reader to understand what comes next—the explanation of the cost—while keeping in mind the purpose of the "toil," "help," and "sacrifice": the "splendid blessings of peace."

Franklin D. Roosevelt, Third Inaugural Address, January 20, 1941 (p. 92)

1. The dashes in this passage serve as markers to indicate amplification. The text that comes after the dashes explains and illustrates the words that come before the dashes. They also indicate a pause for thought (a common convention in speeches). Roosevelt could have used colons here, but dashes are more informal and conversational, producing the effect Roosevelt would want in a speech to all Americans.

2. The parallel structure of this passage emphasizes the simile ("a nation, like a person"). Just as a person has a body, mind, and spirit, so does a nation. The parallel structure of the speech echoes the parallels between a person and a nation. The structure also makes the passage more memorable, emphasizing the idea that a nation must be cared for just like a person.

Robert Snedden, *Adaptation and Survival* (p. 93)

1. The purpose of the dash is to set off and emphasize the "amazing sense of smell" bears have. What follows the dash is parenthetical since this passage is not a comparison of bears and other animals. The parenthetical thought is just an intensifier. The dash is also an informal punctuation mark. Here Snedden is talking to the reader. The tone is friendly and conversational. This is also the purpose of the exclamation point in sentence three. The exclamation point shows enthusiasm, even amazement, pointing out just how amazing a bear's sense of smell is and bringing the reader into the conversation (with the hope that the reader will find the details amazing too).

2. Informational text usually contains sentences that are clear, with no unusual word order. This relates to the writer's purpose. With informational text, the purpose is to explain or inform, and clarity is highly valued, thus the straightforward sentences. More literary text often strives for complexity, suggestion, and multiple meanings. This purpose is better served by sentences that are themselves complex and experimental.

Louisa May Alcott, *Little Women* (p. 94)

1. The subject of the sentence is "weeks." The main verb is "were." This is not the usual order of subjects and verbs in English. In a declarative sentence, the subject usually comes first and the verb follows the subject.

2. First, the unusual word order catches the reader's attention and places emphasis on the sentence. Also, the word order moves the weight of the sentence to the end, as the reader must read on to find out the subject of the sentence. This draws attention to the weeks and slows down the sentence, like the "peaceful weeks" the sentence describes.

Rudyard Kipling, *The Jungle Book* (p. 95)

1. The short sentence presents the main idea and prepares the reader for the development that follows. Using a short sentence for the main idea expedites reading by setting a purpose for the reader. It focuses the reader's attention and sets up the structure: main idea followed by detail and development.

2. The form of the second sentence echoes its meaning. The sentence is as breathless as the seal's experiment with swimming. There are four clauses in the sentence, all connected by the conjunction "and." By stringing clauses that are connected by the same conjunction with only an occasional comma, Kipling creates a feeling of movement, a feeling similar to a series of waves. The seal tries to swim and is swept under each time. In the same way, the reader tries to fully comprehend (and finish) the sentence but is swept into the sequence of clauses. Form imitates meaning here.

Lyndon Baines Johnson, Remarks at the University of Michigan, May 22, 1964 (p. 96)

1. Johnson starts with a clear, short declarative sentence. He establishes his main contention about the Great Society: that it rests on "abundance and liberty for all." The short sentence states his focus, his claim. The rest of the passage develops his claim, and syntax helps him make his point. In the first paragraph, Johnson starts a sentence pattern that he will continue throughout: "it is…," "it demands…," "it is not…" (all referring to the Great Society). This sentence pattern continually focuses the reader's attention on the Great Society, its meaning, and its promise. Johnson ends the first paragraph with a very short sentence that begins with a conjunction, "but." Although students are often taught not to start a sentence with a conjunction, it is perfectly fine if not overused. "But" indicates an opposing idea and here jolts the reader into the knowledge that ending poverty and racial injustice is not enough. There is more to come. In the second paragraph, Johnson continues the sentence pattern that intensifies the reader's focus on what the Great Society is and is not. The third paragraph again begins with a conjunction, "but." Here the conjunction connects the paragraph to the central concern with what the Great Society is and is not, but it deemphasizes the preceding development and offers a contrary claim: that there is something more important than everything that has been said. Johnson goes back to the "it is…," "it is not…" pattern with a layered sentence. He layers four noun phrases, focusing the reader's attention on what the Great Society is not. Then he goes back to the positive ("it is…"), leaving the reader with a positive impression of the ultimate destiny of the Great Society.

2. The speech would lack interest, focus, and strength. No one would remember anything about it. General, abstract statements without detail or interesting syntax hold no power to engage an audience or a reader.

Mark Twain, "The Weather," Address at the New England Society's Seventy First Annual Dinner, New York City, *Speeches of Mark Twain*, part 1 (p. 102)

1. The tone of the passage is humorous and satirical. Several other words could apply, but students do need to understand that the essay is funny, mocking New England weather. (Also, see if they catch the political satire: "you'd think it was something valuable, and a Congressman had been there.") Students should come up with tone words of their own. It is important for students to keep an active list of tone words and to add to them as they build proficiency in analyzing tone.

2. The tone of the passage is understood from the elements of voice working together. The chart will form the foundation for discussing how the passage builds tone. There are many examples, but charts should look something like this:

Diction What specific words help create the tone?	Detail What details add to the tone?	Figurative Language What figures of speech help create the tone?	Imagery What images help create the tone?	Syntax How does the sentence structure help create the tone?
"gems" "fix up" "sally out" "inhuman perversity of the New England weather"	"the earthquake is due; you stand from under, and take hold of something to steady yourself, and the first thing you know you get struck by lightning"	"brightest gems in the New England weather" (metaphor, ironic) "drowned" (hyperbole) "the thunder begins to merely tune up and scrape and saw, and key up the instruments for the performance"; "the baton is raised (implied personification—figurative term is a conductor) and the real concert begins" (extended metaphor)	"you'll find that stranger down in the cellar with his head in the ash-barrel" "I like to hear rain on a tin roof!"	dash to break the thought and introduce the political satire fragment ("And the thunder.") to add emphasis variety of sentence lengths direct address to the audience short sentences at the end to confirm the perversity of New England weather

Mark Twain, "The Weather," Address at the New England Society's Seventy First Annual Dinner, New York City, *Speeches of Mark Twain*, part 2 (p. 104)

1. The tone here is totally different from the first part of the speech. Here the tone is admiring, awestruck, and reverent. Students should add any new tone words to their charts.

2. Twain shifts his attention from the negative aspects of weather to the dazzlingly beautiful: autumn foliage and the ice storm. The satire is gone, and he creates an unforgettable picture of stark and breathtaking beauty. The transition that marks the change is "there is [*sic*] at least one or two things about that weather (or, if you please, effects produced by it) which we residents would not like to part with." I have indicated below the diction, detail, imagery, and figurative language that help create the tone:

Mind, in this speech I have been trying merely to do honor to the New England weather— no language could do it justice. But, after all, there is [sic] at least one or two things about that weather (or, if you please, effects produced by it) which we residents would not like to part with. If we hadn't our bewitching autumn foliage (diction), we should still have to credit (diction) the weather with one feature which compensates for all its bullying vagaries (personification; diction)—the ice-storm: when a leafless tree is clothed (personification; imagery) with ice from the bottom to the top—ice that is as bright and clear as crystal (simile; also imagery and detail); when every bough and twig is strung with ice-beads (metaphor), frozen dew-drops, and the whole tree sparkles cold and white (imagery, detail), like the Shah of Persia's diamond plume (simile). Then the wind waves (diction) the branches and the sun comes out and turns all those myriads (diction) of beads and drops to prisms that glow and burn and flash with all manner of colored fires, which change and change again with inconceivable rapidity from blue to red, from red to green, and green to gold (metaphor; imagery; detail)—the tree becomes a spraying fountain, a very explosion of dazzling jewels (simile; imagery; detail); and it stands there the acme, the climax, the supremest possibility in art or nature, of bewildering, intoxicating, intolerable magnificence (diction). One cannot make the words too strong.

The syntax also helps create the tone. The dashes amplify ideas and indicate coming examples or clarification. The long, layered sentences provide detail and support for the "bullying vagaries" of New England weather. The dashes amplify ideas and indicate coming examples or that the beauty of the ice storm compensates for the "bullying vagaries" of New England weather. The short sentence at the end of the speech emphasizes the seriousness of his description and validates the stunning beauty of the ice storm.

William Shakespeare, *The Tempest* (p. 105)

1. The tone of the passage (and the attitude of the speaker) is one of awe and enthusiasm. This is expressed by the diction ("O, wonder," "goodly creatures," "beauteous," "brave new world") and the syntax (use of exclamation points and the use of exclamatory sentence structure with its inversion of typical word order).

2. The tone flattens, and the passage loses its enthusiasm and awe. In addition, changing the second line to a question casts doubt as to whether there are many goodly creatures at all. The important point to make is that punctuation is a powerful writing tool that helps writers express voice. It is also important to remind students not to overuse exclamation points. Their effect lies in their careful and specialized use. Although Shakespeare uses several in this passage, in general he uses them sparingly.

Booker T. Washington, *Up From Slavery: An Autobiography* (p. 106)

1. Considering the topic and content, one would expect the tone to be angry and vengeful. However, the tone here is dispassionate and objective. The tone frees the reader to enter into the experience, gather the details of the experience, and try to understand Washington's perspective.

2. The syntax is straightforward, with strong, declarative sentences. This helps set the objective tone of the passage. In addition, the sentences are short and easily understood, setting the clear, dispassionate tone. The short sentence that begins with a conjunction ("But I do not find especial fault with him.") reinforces the tone of objective acceptance, both in content and form. (The conjunction "but" indicates a contrary idea. Although the father here is not worthy of the "father" designation, Washington does not find fault. Instead, he views this "father" as another victim of slavery.)

Ambrose Bierce, *The Devil's Dictionary* (p. 107)

1. "Obsolete" means outdated, no longer used. Bierce's definition is less a definition than a criticism of "fool writers." According to Bierce, only foolish writers avoid obsolete words if they are good words. A good writer uses a word deemed obsolete by the dictionary if there is "no modern equivalent equally good."

2. Bierce's attitude toward words being defined as obsolete is disdainful and mocking. He is clearly no fan of lexicographers as the judge of a word's usefulness. He states that things obsolete are "no longer used by the timid," implying that those who eschew the obsolete are fearful, faint-hearted followers. Obsolete words are objects of "dread and loathing to the fool writer," to be avoided at all cost. But an obsolete word is good enough for the good writer "if it is a good word and has no exact modern equivalent equally good." In other words, good writers judge words on their merit not based on what another authority says. His diction reveals his attitude: "timid," "dread," "loathing," "fool," "good" (repeated four times).

Abraham Lincoln, "From an Address to an Indiana Regiment. March 17, 1865," *Speeches and Letters of Abraham Lincoln, 1832–1865* (p. 108)

1. Lincoln is totally opposed to slavery and finds it abhorrent. He conveys his attitude through a mild and pleasant tone that belies his vehement opposition to slavery. His claim is that "all men (people) should be free"—straightforward enough. Then he gives his conditions for allowing the possibility of slavery: that the only people who should be slaves are those who want to have slaves for themselves or those who want other people to have slaves. His stated argument is not passionate or heated. Instead, his argument is calm, logical, and convincing. His diction is not elaborate or condemning. It is controlled and plain. His final statement sums up his argument: that anyone arguing for slavery should try being a slave. By understating his opposition to slavery, Lincoln points out both the absurdity and the horror of slavery.

2. The tone changes to an almost whiny and confrontational one, and the power of the passage is lost. The power of the original passage lies in its cool logic and underlying passion. This passage sounds spiteful rather than logical, puts readers on the defensive, and thus loses its power to convince.

Lewis Carroll, *Alice's Adventures in Wonderland* (p. 109)

1. The attitude that underlies the argument is clear: Word order does matter a great deal (in English, of course). The reader knows this from following the detailed remarks of the Hatter, March Hare, and the Dormouse. Obviously, switching the word order changes the meaning. Precision of language and meaning matter. The examples are funny but relentless, with one example coming after another in rapid succession, reinforced by the repetition of the introductory clause ("You might just as well say…"). Alice's careless remark ("that's the same thing, you know") is quickly dismissed.

2. The tone of the passage is both humorous and critical. Carroll creates the tone through diction, detail, and syntax. The characters are funny, as is the chaotic dialogue—jumping from one thing to another. But underlying the humor is the belief and demonstration that language matters: Word order matters, diction matters, and precision of meaning is not something to dismiss lightly.

Jen Green, *The Impact of Environmentalism: Food and Farming* (p. 110)

1. The author's attitude toward supermarkets is negative. The diction reveals the attitude in this passage: supermarkets "undercut one another's prices"; supermarkets make things "difficult for farmers, both in developing countries and in the developed world"; "farmers have been forced out of business"; prices are "ultra-low"; standards are "very high" and must be met or food is "rejected"; rejected food "leads to enormous waste." Although this is an informational piece, the attitude that underlies the instruction is clearly on the side of the farmer and against the practices of supermarkets.

2. The tone of the passage is complicated. This is informational text. As such, the tone is usually objective and instructive. In this passage, the tone does seem objective and instructive. However, on closer examination, there is a strong bias against supermarkets in favor of the farmer. This sets a tone that is both instructive and critical. The diction associated with supermarkets is almost all negative, as described in #1 above. The only positive comment is that the undercutting of prices is "good for shoppers." Details also support the tone. The price war is "to increase their share of trade"; the low prices affect "developing countries" and the "developed world"; "many farmers have been forced out of business"; fruits and vegetables must be "of an exact size and shape…free of all blemishes.…" The syntax is straightforward, with clear, declarative sentences. This reinforces the instructive tone of the passage. The last sentence is short and direct. There is nothing ambiguous about it. It instructs, but it instructs with an underlying tone of criticism.

John F. Kennedy, Inaugural Address, January 20, 1961 (p. 111)

1. The tone of this passage is serious, passionate, and dignified. There are many tone words that could describe these famous lines. This is a good opportunity for students to increase their tone vocabulary.

2. Students' charts should look something like this:

Syntax	How it shapes the tone
Starting the first sentence with "And so."	It sets a conversational tone and connects the idea that follows to the previous ideas in the speech.
The colon in the first sentence	It indicates that something important is to follow. It also indicates a direct address to his audience, Americans.
The reversal of the usual word order ("ask not" instead of "do not ask")	It is emphatic. It focuses the reader's attention on the "not asking" and the "asking" and shifts the reader's attention to what should be his or her concern.
The dash in the first sentence	It indicates a change in thought. It also sets an informal and conversational tone.
The colon in the second sentence	It serves the same function as the colon in the first sentence. However, here Kennedy broadens his plea and addresses the "citizens of the world."
Sentence length	The length of the two sentences is comparable, as is their structure. This reinforces the parallel nature of the sentences, giving equal importance to both ideas.

Frances Hodgson Burnett, *The Secret Garden* (p. 112)

1. The tone of this passage is exuberant and high spirited. Students should brainstorm additional words to describe the tone and add these words to their list.

2. Diction helps create the tone of exuberance: she "panted"; we could "slip" through the door; we could make the garden "come alive." Detail, imagery, and figurative language reinforce the tone: "no one knows but ourselves" (detail); "door, hidden somewhere under the ivy" (detail and imagery); "no one knew anyone was inside" (detail); "we were missel thrushes and it was our nest" (metaphor); "dug and planted seeds and made it all come alive" (detail and imagery). The syntax of this passage strongly reinforces the tone. The dashes indicate a conversational informality and a breathlessness of loosely connected thought. The entire passage is one sentence, with thoughts connected only by dashes, commas, and semicolons. This syntax imitates the exuberance of the character's speech—she is so excited that she cannot even take time to catch her breath with a period. Also, the conditional word "if" is repeated five times in the sentence, echoing the fact that although her plans are not yet actuality, the speaker is relentlessly intending to make her plans reality.

Standards Correlations

The lessons in this book are correlated to the Common Core State Standards for Reading, Writing, Speaking & Listening, and Language for grades six through ten.

Common Core Anchor Standards	Lessons
CCSS.ELA-Literacy.CCRA.R.1: Read closely to determine what the text says explicitly and to make logical inferences from it; cite specific textual evidence when writing or speaking to support conclusions drawn from the text.	All lessons
CCSS.ELA-Literacy.CCRA.R.2: Determine central ideas or themes of a text and analyze their development; summarize the key supporting details and ideas.	All Detail lessons (pp. 25–38) All Tone lessons (pp. 99–114)
CCSS.ELA-Literacy.CCRA.R.4: Interpret words and phrases as they are used in a text, including determining technical, connotative, and figurative meanings, and analyze how specific word choices shape meaning or tone.	All lessons
CCSS.ELA-Literacy.CCRA.R.5: Analyze the structure of texts, including how specific sentences, paragraphs, and larger portions of the text (e.g., a section, chapter, scene, or stanza) relate to each other and the whole.	All Syntax lessons (pp. 83–98) All Tone lessons (pp. 99–114)
CCSS.ELA-Literacy.CCRA.R.6: Assess how point of view or purpose shapes the content and style of a text.	All Tone lessons (pp. 99–114)
CCSS.ELA-Literacy.CCRA.R.10: Read and comprehend complex literary and informational texts independently and proficiently.	All lessons
CCSS.ELA-Literacy.CCRA.W.3: Write narratives to develop real or imagined experiences or events using effective technique, well-chosen details, and well-structured event sequences.	All Detail lessons (pp. 25–38) All Imagery lessons (pp. 70–82) All Tone lessons (pp. 99–114)
CCSS.ELA-Literacy.CCRA.W.4: Produce clear and coherent writing in which the development, organization, and style are appropriate to task, purpose, and audience.	All "Now you try it" exercises
CCSS.ELA-Literacy.CCRA.W.5: Develop and strengthen writing as needed by planning, revising, editing, rewriting, or trying a new approach.	All "Now you try it" exercises, especially trying a new approach
CCSS.ELA-Literacy.CCRA.W.9: Draw evidence from literary or informational texts to support analysis, reflection, and research.	All lessons
CCSS.ELA-Literacy.CCRA.W.10: Write routinely over extended time frames (time for research, reflection, and revision) and shorter time frames (a single sitting or a day or two) for a range of tasks, purposes, and audiences.	All "Now you try it" exercises
CCSS.ELA-Literacy.CCRA.SL.1: Prepare for and participate effectively in a range of conversations and collaborations with diverse partners, building on others' ideas and expressing their own clearly and persuasively.	All lessons
CCSS.ELA-Literacy.CCRA.L.1: Demonstrate command of the conventions of standard English grammar and usage when writing or speaking.	All Syntax lessons (pp. 83–98)

CCSS.ELA-Literacy.CCRA.L.2: Demonstrate command of the conventions of standard English capitalization, punctuation, and spelling when writing.	All Syntax lessons (pp. 83–98)
CCSS.ELA-Literacy.CCRA.L.3: Apply knowledge of language to understand how language functions in different contexts, to make effective choices for meaning or style, and to comprehend more fully when reading or listening.	All lessons
CCSS.ELA-Literacy.CCRA.L.4: Determine or clarify the meaning of unknown and multiple-meaning words and phrases by using context clues, analyzing meaningful word parts, and consulting general and specialized reference materials, as appropriate.	All Diction lessons (pp. 10–24) All Imagery lessons (pp. 70–82)
CCSS.ELA-Literacy.CCRA.L.5: Demonstrate understanding of figurative language, word relationships, and nuances in word meanings.	All Diction lessons (pp. 10–24) All Figurative Language lessons (pp. 39–69) All Imagery lessons (pp. 70–82)

Index of Authors and Titles

37. Lincoln, Abraham, "From an Address to an Indiana Regiment," *Speeches and Letters of Abraham Lincoln, 1832–1865* (p. 108)

38. Lincoln, Abraham, The Gettysburg Address (p. 44)

39. London, Jack, *The Call of the Wild* (pp. 16, 52)

40. McClure, Alexander K., *Lincoln's Yarns and Stories* (p. 37)

41. Melville, Herman, *Moby-Dick; or, The Whale* (p. 72)

42. Noyes, Alfred, "The Highwayman" (p. 43)

43. O. Henry, "The Lonesome Road," *41 Stories by O. Henry* (p. 20)

44. O. Henry, "The Ransom of Red Chief" (p. 29)

45. Oxlade, Chris, *Storm Warning: Tornadoes* (Capstone, 2005) (pp. 21, 75)

46. Poe, Edgar Allan, "The Raven" (p. 24)

47. Poe, Edgar Allan, "The Tell-Tale Heart," *The Tell-Tale Heart and Other Writings* (p. 89)

48. Queen Elizabeth I, Speech to the Troops at Tilbury (p. 63)

49. Roosevelt, Franklin D., First Inaugural Address (pp. 30, 97)

50. Roosevelt, Franklin D., Third Inaugural Address (p. 92)

51. Roosevelt, Theodore, *An Autobiography* (p. 37)

52. Roosevelt, Theodore, *Letters to His Children* (p. 81)

53. Sandburg, Carl, "How the Five Rusty Rats Helped Find a New Village," *Rootabaga Stories* (p. 12)

54. Sewell, Anna, *Black Beauty* (p. 81)

55. Shakespeare, William, *As You Like It* (p. 46)

56. Shakespeare, William, *Henry IV, Part II* (p. 61)

57. Shakespeare, William, *Macbeth* (p. 68)

58. Shakespeare, William, *Romeo and Juliet* (pp. 69, 114)

59. Shakespeare, William, *The Tempest* (p. 105)

60. Shaw, George Bernard, *Pygmalion* (p. 49)

61. Shelley, Mary Wollstonecraft, *Frankenstein* (p. 88)

62. Shelley, Percy Bysshe, "Ozymandias" (p. 65)

63. Snedden, Robert, *Adaptation and Survival* (Capstone, 2012) (pp. 23, 93)

64. Snedden, Robert, *DNA and Genetic Engineering* (Capstone, 2008) (p. 47)

65. Solway, Andrew, *The Impact of Environmentalism: Transportation* (Capstone, 2013) (p. 37)

66. Spilsbury, Richard, *Managing Water* (Capstone, 2009) (pp. 28, 79, 97, 113)

67. Spyri, Johanna, *Heidi* (p. 76)

68. Stevenson, Robert Louis, *Treasure Island* (p. 32)

69. Twain, Mark, *The Adventures of Huckleberry Finn* (p. 73)

70. Twain, Mark, *The Adventures of Tom Sawyer* (p. 60)

71. Twain, Mark, "The Weather," Address at the New England Society's Seventy First Annual Dinner, *Speeches of Mark Twain* (pp. 102, 104)

72. Verne, Jules, *Around the World in Eighty Days* (p. 15)

73. Washington, Booker T., *Up from Slavery: An Autobiography* (pp. 80, 106)

74. Wells, H. G., *The Invisible Man* (p. 38)

75. Wells, H. G., *The Time Machine* (p. 45)

● Maupin House *by*

capstone®
professional

At Maupin House by Capstone Professional, we continue to look for professional development resources that support grades K–8 classroom teachers in areas, such as these:

Literacy	Language Arts
Content-Area Literacy	Research-Based Practices
Assessment	Inquiry
Technology	Differentiation
Standards-Based Instruction	School Safety
Classroom Management	School Community

If you have an idea for a professional development resource, visit our Become an Author website at:

http://maupinhouse.com/index.php/become-an-author

There are two ways to submit questions and proposals.

1. You may send them electronically to:
   http://maupinhouse.com/index.php/become-an-author

2. You may send them via postal mail. Please be sure to include a self-addressed stamped envelope for us to return materials.

   Acquisitions Editor
   Capstone Professional
   1 N. LaSalle Street, Suite 1800
   Chicago, IL 60602